The Design and Construction of The British Library

Watercolour study of the Entrance Hall by the author. (Coll. Avery Library)

The Design and Construction of The British Library

Colin St John Wilson

The British Library
1998

This book is dedicated to all book lovers
but especially to my brother Peter
whose library in a tower was the magic
lair of my schooldays

Contents

Preface

At 9.30 am on Monday 24 November 1997 at St Pancras the doors of The British Library opened to some 80 members of the public who had been queuing outside. As they crossed the threshold to become part of one of the most important days in the Library's history most gasped in astonishment at the sight.

There had been criticism of the decision to leave the splendours of the British Museum but within days the Library's readers had settled in and began to get used to the convenience and efficiency of the new arrangements. The North Reading Room in the Museum building, a favourite haunt of the regular readers, was due to remain open until the end of February 1998. But the readers voted with their feet. Within a few weeks that reading room was deserted and it was quietly closed without notice or comment, a month early.

For the Library works superbly well. Books can be located quickly; delivered safely and speedily; read in comfort and then returned without fuss. There is a quiet air of friendly joint endeavour between readers and staff, an air of purposeful industry in the Humanities Reading Room that is a joy to experience.

All of us who use and work in the Library owe an enormous debt of gratitude to Sandy Wilson and the Design Team for having provided us with the gentle, welcoming, ambience which makes all of that possible. The new building is a fitting tribute to the vision of those who in 1972 created The British Library and who wished to provide a single home, not only for the magnificent heritage from the Museum, but also for the patents and scientific journals and the ongoing flood of the results of the world's research and scholarly communities, in whatever form it may be published.

But our new building belongs not just to us but to the nation. As citizens I think we can also be grateful to Sandy Wilson for his success in creating a building that does such credit to our times. With great determination he has overcome the financial and bureaucratic obstacles that public authorities seem too often to place in the way of those who wish to create lasting monuments for us. He has designed not only a superb library but a showcase for British sculpture, tapestry and art generally. As they cross the threshold visitors will continue to gasp, whether they come as tourists to see the exhibitions of our treasures or as readers to consult the 12 million books housed on the shelves. That is as it should be. I can think of no more fitting way to signal the start of the Information Age.

Dr JOHN ASHWORTH
Chairman, The British Library Board

Introduction

There are certain types of building over which there hovers an aura of myth. The most transcendent of all, the cathedral, is grounded in the sacred so that both form and pattern of use are fused in the language of ritual. But there is one type of building which is profane yet in fulfilling its proper role touches the hem of the sacred: the great library. One has only to think of what crowds into the mind when we recall the destruction of the Library in Alexandria or, akin to that fire, the blasphemy that underlay the burning of the books by Nazi decree, for one to be made aware that the library and what it houses embodies and protects the freedom and diversity of the human spirit in a way that borders on the sacred. And so to someone brought up in a den of books in a family one half of which were publishers and writers the idea of building a great library has always been (next to a cathedral!) the most haunting of ambitions. It was so for me.

I have had the good fortune to pursue that dream (not without moments of nightmare) into reality. It has taken thirty-six years (although I once, in a fit of optimism, called it my 'Thirty Years War') to get to the point at which we can celebrate completion of at least its major core: and I am now both touched and grateful to be invited to give some account of the building and how it came into being.

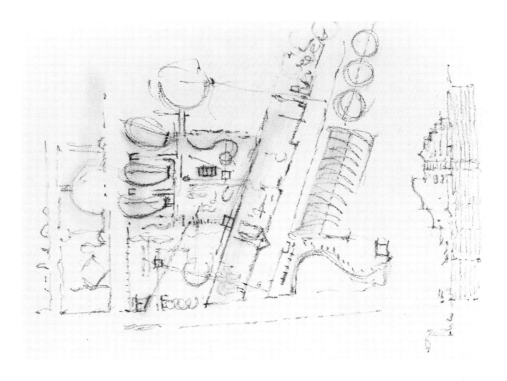

St Pancras Site: forms and themes.
(Drawing by Wilson)

A National Library viewed in more pragmatic terms is a day-to-day workplace as well as an institution that embodies and celebrates the collective memory of the nation. But as the storehouse from which not only traditional scholarship but also the new information technologies will draw their primary source material it increasingly takes on new powers both economically and politically. Uniquely among national institutions it has to represent and serve both that which is most ancient and that which is most ebulliently in a state of growth and development.

The greater part of space in such a building will inevitably be dedicated to places of study and the storage of the collections; but it has also the duty to put on exhibition to both scholars and the general public its treasures which are of great beauty or special historic significance. To catch the imagination of the young as well as to tease the erudition of the student the range of material to be drawn upon is unique – Persian miniatures and illuminated manuscripts, Magna Carta, Handel's 'Messiah', 'Alice's Adventures Underground' and Nelson's battle-plan to his captains at Trafalgar. Further still, the mandate of the Library is extended to encompass the world of academic discourse in lecture and seminar in its own centre for conferences and in the department dedicated to wider educational services. Finally, 'back of house', space and facilities have to be found for conservation laboratories, acquisition and cataloguing departments, photographic studios, administration and general amenities.

Each of these different centres of activity have their own working pattern and we will explore them in some detail in due course. But all of them are answerable to a number of general considerations in the field of design philosophy such as the historical and physical context of the project, strategies for coping with the factors of growth and change, and, hovering over any institution of such importance, the question of symbolic and representational form and its appropriate incorporation in visual works of art.

I have been asked to give an account not only of what the new building is but also of the design process by which it came into being. Where the casual observer tends to talk about what a building 'looks like' the architect is most concerned to discover what the building 'wants to be' and how it will 'work'. Perhaps therefore an account of the design principles and methods that we have used will be of some general interest. But first a word or two about the history and politics of the venture.

The Historical Background

'The Thirty Years War'

'This job may take quite a long time to get done' muttered the Chairman of the Selection Committee that appointed Sir Leslie Martin and me to design the new library for the British Museum in 1962. He was a gentleman who looked like Sydney Greenstreet in 'The Maltese Falcon' and a hooded but steely eye seemed to be calculating the odds on my chances of attaining the necessary longevity. His findings appeared to re-assure him.

That was thirty-six years ago and it is the only comment upon the Library that has held unchallengeably true ever since.

The Trustees of the British Museum had set out to implement the proposal put forward in the 1951 County of London Plan to relocate the Museum's Library and Department of Prints & Drawings on land to the south of the Museum between Great Russell Street and Bloomsbury Way.

The method of selection for an architect was competitive interview and the choice fell upon Professor Sir Leslie Martin and myself, largely, I believe, on the evidence of

British Museum Library Project (1962–4). A grand plaza over Great Russell Street connects the British Museum directly to Hawksmoor's St George's Church with the Library sited to the right and, to the left, the Department of Prints & Drawings backing onto a residential complex with peripheral shops and offices. (© Mann)

British Museum Library Project (1962–4). Floor plan at the level of the L-shaped Catalogue Hall that lies between the large General Reading Room and the six special Departmental Reading Rooms. A Reference Reading Room for the general public lies, top left, between the two points of entrance. (Drawing by Wilson)

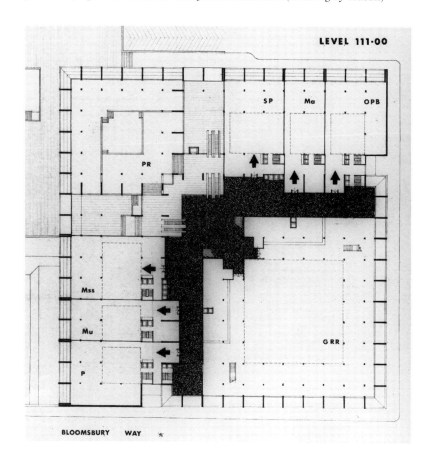

the group of three libraries for the University that we had built in Manor Road, Oxford.

The Museum Brief was expanded to embrace a mixed development of residential, commercial and office use to compensate for the property to be demolished; and a design was completed by mid-1964. Its principal feature, made possible by the projected closure of Great Russell Street, was a broad plaza connecting the Museum directly to the new development and the church of St George Bloomsbury, designed by Nicholas Hawksmoor.

The eastern half of the site was allocated to the Library building. Square in plan, this was dominated by a three-floor-high terraced Reading Room, flanked on two sides (west & north) by the six Departmental Reading Rooms (Maps, Manuscripts, State Papers, Periodicals, Oriental & Music Collections). Lying in the L-shape interspace between the base of the major Reading Room and the six Departmental Reading

W. R. Lethaby's proposal in 1891 for a 'Sacred Way' from the British Museum to old Waterloo Bridge. It should be 'wisely extravagant, wide, full of trees ... and would almost alone give an organic system to London'.

Rooms was the Catalogue Hall over which the stepped-terraces of the Reading Room loomed like a ship in dry dock. The open northwest sector of the space which constituted the Entrance Hall embraced a large Reading Room dedicated to the general public for reference purposes.

The major part of the collections were to be stored in seven floors (four of which were below ground) under the Reading Rooms in a deep space whose external perimeter above ground housed the offices of the various Departmental Collections.

The design had a certain grand simplicity, square in plan and symmetrical about the N-W / S-E diagonal but it would have had to be constructed all at once and would have afforded little opportunity to take aboard any change and none to allow for growth.

It is perhaps of interest to note (in the light of subsequent controversy) that at that time there was no protest at the proposal to evacuate the Round Reading Room. In a subsequent Report to the Trustees on 'The Short and Long-term Development of the Museum' I observed that that Room was based (within 3 feet) upon the Pantheon in Rome and should ideally be adapted to fulfil that (badly needed) function for the Museum by opening up its centre to easy access from north and south.

To the west stood St George's Church, now freestanding for the first time, and beyond it the Department of Prints & Drawings. The rest of the land to the west was allocated to a residential development for 350 people distributed in terraced form around a central green space with 3,000 sq.m. of commercial space and 2,000 sq.m. of office accommodation tucked in around the perimeter together with a couple of public houses.

It is interesting to recall the proposal put forward by Lethaby for the opening up of a grand route and vista southwards all the way to the Embankment, but even in the bold 'Sixties' such grandeur could not be revived.

The scheme was approved by the Tory Government in 1964. However the incoming Labour Government was very responsive to the growing conservationist campaign to preserve Bloomsbury while, at the same time, the terms of reference for

British Museum Library Project (1962–4). Cross-section showing the Catalogue Hall, centre, over which the large General Reading Room steps in terrace form with the adjacent Music Department on the left. The Collections are stored in seven floors below with departmental and other offices distributed around the perimeter. (Drawing by Wilson)

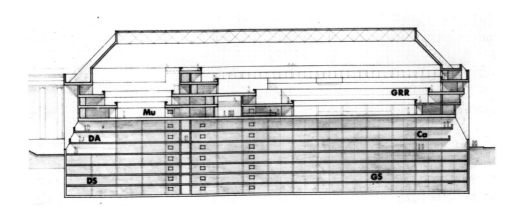

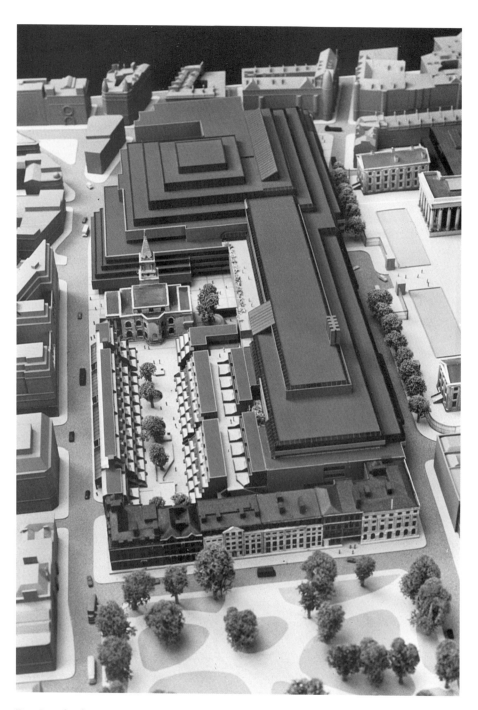

First British Library Project (1972). Model showing the site reduced by the listing of the Bloomsbury Square frontage and now required to accommodate the addition of the Science Collections (right foreground). A residential avenue is centred on St George's Church behind which lie the Humanities Collections. Great Russell Street and the British Museum forecourt remain unchanged.

the Library were undergoing scrutiny from the Dainton Committee. With a view to uniting all but the Newspaper Collections in one place, the Science & Patents Departments were called in to join the Humanities Collections of the Museum and the concept of a single national library began to emerge. I was commissioned to explore the feasibility of accommodating such a complex on the Bloomsbury site, Sir Leslie Martin having withdrawn from the fray by this time; and parallel with these studies the concept of a single national library moved towards its political realization to become established by Act of Parliament in 1972.

Three major changes in circumstance over the original Museum scheme raised serious problems right from the start. In the first place, to bring the Science & Patents Departments to the site resulted in a doubling of the accommodation to be housed there. Secondly the site area had by now been reduced in size by the decision to preserve the whole of the west side of Bloomsbury Square. Thirdly the planning authority would concede little reduction in the amount of residential development to be replaced on the site.

The predictable result was that the design that emerged was massively over-crowded and together with the increasing strength of the conservationist campaign led to the decision in 1973 to look for an alternative site. For this purpose nine of the twelve acres to be vacated by British Rail in Somerstown St Pancras were acquired for the project.

After intensive exploration of alternative design strategies the new proposal evolved quite swiftly and was attended with much goodwill. The Royal Fine Art Commission applauded it as 'a brilliant solution to a very complex problem' and it was formally approved by the Secretary of State for Education (Shirley Williams) in 1978.

The following year, with yet another change of government, all was at risk once more. There were rumours of fierce battles in high places and but for the valiant championship of the first two Chairmen of the Board (Lord Eccles and Sir Fred, later Lord Dainton) the whole project would have foundered.

Powerful forces were marshalled against it. A very understandable nostalgia for the famous Round Reading Room of the British Museum fuelled a last-ditch battle for its retention; an equally understandable disgust at much so-called 'Sixties' architecture was alarmingly transformed into an inexplicable call for a stylistic retreat into the 18th century; and finally, the conjunction of these two prejudices gave an extra fillip to the fashion of the day in right-wing circles to 'think the unthinkable'. Although much of this revealed no great talent for thinking, much of it did issue from sources heavily supported in the public domain of press and television. That the project has finally survived onslaught from three such quarters (not to mention some well-advertised problems in carrying out the construction) must surely be proof of its fundamental necessity.

The fact that twelve years' work and two whole projects in Bloomsbury came to nothing is a sorry tale. However the ensuing relocation of site to St Pancras has

proved to be enormously to the advantage of the Library, for two main reasons. First, the Bloomsbury site was never going to be large enough to allow for growth and change in the future. This inevitable contingency was one of the essential grounds for choosing the St Pancras site where the necessary additional land was indeed purchased to allow for growth after a first phase of construction. Secondly the status of the area would undergo significant transformation if the current intention to site the Channel Tunnel Terminal at St Pancras were to be carried out. For then the Library would be the first building to greet the visitor and the Piazza, which is the only large public space in the vicinity, would become the threshold to and from Europe, over and above its role as a place of relaxation for visitors to the Library.

The British Library at St Pancras. Perspective view of the north-east corner of the Library. (Drawing by Wilson)

Design Method

The English Free School

The design principles which have motivated this project are grounded in a body of work known as the English Free School which came to birth around the middle of the 19th century. It was generated in response to the need for public buildings of increasing complexity of every type – law courts, hospitals, railway stations, municipal and commercial headquarters, museums, libraries and schools. Whereas the established theory of design (as epitomised in the famous teaching of the Beaux-Arts School) tried to shoe-horn this diversity into the procrustean formulae of 'Classical' symmetries a group of architects in England (Butterfield & Pugin, Waterhouse & Street, Burgess & Scott) took as their model the free asymmetries of an organic nature.

William Butterfield:
All Saints, Margaret Street, London
(1850–9).

The sense in which the word 'organic' is used here is that of Samuel Taylor Coleridge:

'The form is mechanic when on any given material we impose a pre-determined form, not necessarily arising out of the properties of the material, as when to a mass of wet clay we give whatever shape we wish it to retain when hardened. The organic form, on the other hand, is innate; it shapes as it develops itself from within, and the fullness of its development is one and the same with the perfection of its outward form. Such is the life, such is the form.'

The roots of this School lay in the freedom of Gothic form. In the words of the great spokesman of the group, John Ruskin: 'Gothic is not only the best but the only rational architecture, as being that which can fit itself most easily to all services, vulgar or noble. It can shrink into a turret, expand into a hall, coil into a staircase or spring into a spire, with undegraded grace and unexhausted energy; and whenever it finds occasion for change in its form or purpose, it submits to it without the slightest sense of loss either to its unity or majesty.... And it is one of the virtues of the Gothic builders, that they never suffered ideas of outside symmetries and consistencies to interfere with the real use and value of what they did.'

A further aspect of the historical significance of this School lies in the fact that for the first time a major architectural innovation of international impact was generated from Britain. For its message was quickly transmitted through journals not only in Europe but also to the United States where in the studios of Henry Hobson Richardson, Frank Furness and Frank Lloyd Wright it developed a new energy and wider resources. Wright's 1910 Wasmuth publications in Germany quickly led to wide ramifications in Austria and Germany, Holland and Scandinavia which inspired a new generation of architects after World War I to give the rather arid concept of 'Functionalism' a deeper sense of purpose and a hugely rich repertoire of form – to quote John Ruskin 'subtle and flexible like a fiery serpent but ever attentive to the voice of its charmer.'

Henry Hobson
Richardson:
Library,
Woburn, Mass.
(1876–7)

Frank Lloyd Wright: Robie House,
Chicago (1906).
(© Steinkamp/Ballogg, Chicago)

Alvar Aalto: Saynatsalo Town Hall,
Finland (1952). (© Wilson)

The 'Other Tradition' of Modernism

The essential lesson learnt by the early Modernists from this School is summed up in the phrase 'form follows function'. Unfortunately the first fine rapture all too soon became much reduced to a narrow, mechanistic and pragmatic definition of 'function' with an emphasis upon technology, mass production and avant-garde 'style' for its own sake. This failed to take account of the human, psychological and symbolic elements at play in all of us. However a notable number of that new generation (Aalto, Scharoun, Asplund, Frank Lloyd Wright himself) did form a rebel minority loyal to the original principles in a kind of 'resistance-movement' of its own: and this amounted to a whole 'Other Tradition' within the modern movement.*

In designing the British Library building we have drawn widely upon this tradition not only in the adoption of organic forms that are responsive to growth and change but also in the repertoire of sensuous materials that are particularly responsive to human presence and touch – leather, marble, wood and bronze. We touch, hear and smell a building as much as we see it and furthermore what we do see in terms of weight and texture, density or transparency transmits explicit resonances of a body language that is common to us all but all too seldom consciously addressed.

It is a tradition that unlike the hard-line modernist obsession with 'Progress' never sought to cut itself off from the past or deny itself allusion to precedent and always retained a blood relationship with painting, sculpture and hand-crafts in an age increasingly committed to mechanical reproduction.

Above all it is a tradition that has long-since attained maturity and can justly claim as much authority as the Classical tradition. In the context of a programme of requirements of great complexity and known commitment to growth it is unanswerably appropriate for this project and this site: and the fact that the principal neighbouring building at St Pancras is a spectacular example of the English Free School is a coincidence to be relished.

Working method

The first, and guiding, principle in working within this tradition lies in the conviction that the inspiration must spring from a rigorous factual appreciation of the required conditions and not, as so often the case, the imposition of preconceived forms and ideas upon the real desires and necessities at issue. In the first place therefore the process is one of discovery whose aim is to identify the purposes of the building elements and their interrelationships.

In order to discover what were the 'desires and necessities' of the British Library the architects and a planning group of the Library drew up a Brief to pin down facts wherever we could. Space and environmental standards, working relationships, quantities of equipment and other desiderata were marshalled and tabulated to form a working document.

*cf. my *The Other Tradition*, Academy Editions 1995

It was a rigorous exercise in which, *inter alia*, we had to devise from scratch forms and tabulations to capture the necessary information. Both I and the partner in charge of that operation, M.J. Long, are truly grateful to the individuals in that dedicated team. Given the design process 'from inside out' and given the complexity of the Brief to be addressed it follows that the 'user' client has to be as committed as the architect if the building is truly to serve its proper ends.

For instance the process was no mere checklist but a dialogue that often had an important effect upon the design solution. In trying to put together a design we occasionally found that some specified requirements were shown to be incompatible with others and the solution to these discoveries began to dictate anatomical differences between one part of the building and another.

Consider the following examples:

In open-access reading rooms, the average visit is of short duration, the visitor on the move much of the time, and (relatively) few reading places such as are required

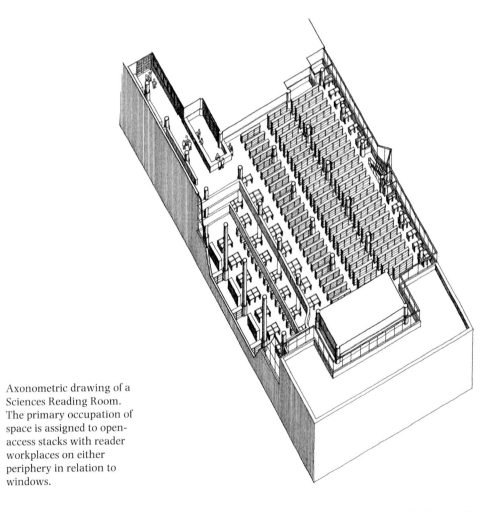

Axonometric drawing of a Sciences Reading Room. The primary occupation of space is assigned to open-access stacks with reader workplaces on either periphery in relation to windows.

are therefore located around the edges of the book collection in 'flexible' space. Because of the dense occupation of space by bookstacks daylight is admitted from the perimeter only.

In the case of closed-access reading rooms, the visit is of long duration. The reader spends most of that time at a single desk, and the material consulted is mostly delivered to it from safe storage elsewhere. Consequently a very different spatial configuration now dedicates the whole of the centre of the space to readers with daylight poured from above through roof lanterns and clerestories.

Two very different patterns of use are therefore served by two very different forms of space. The ensuing asymmetry of western and eastern ranges is played off in the context of an overall warp and woof of common factors and it is in the relative proportioning of these that the characteristic differences lie.

A square structural bay of columns spaced 7.8 m apart is the common underpinning of the whole building. Variety is introduced through the vertical dimension which dictates whether the height of any one bay is the height of a single floor, two floors or three; and it is above all in the capacity of the single floor-height bay to house

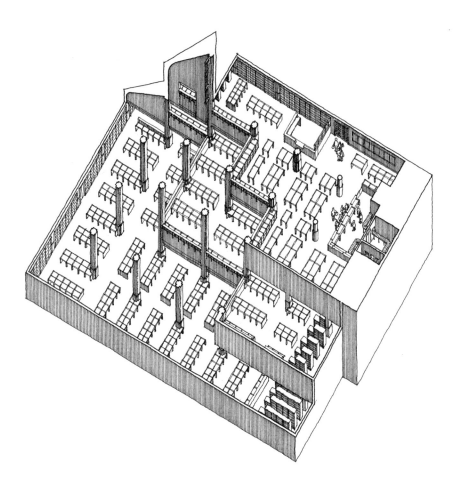

Axonometric drawing of a Humanities Reading Room. The primary occupation of space is assigned to reader workplaces in the centre under rooflights with reference books distributed around the perimeter.

equally well book-stacks, offices and reader workplaces that a certain flexibility is constantly present. This means that however unique some of the soaring double and triple height spaces may be they are always adjacent to bays of single floor height and therefore open to a certain flexibility in their occupation. This adjacency is also further extended by the presence of departmental offices immediately below or above a particular reading room.

It is out of this play of volumetric difference that uniqueness is attended upon by flexibility and it is this factor of workability that has enabled the occupation of the building to be planned in the context of changing priorities enforced by political policy. It will doubtless continue to be an important part of the life of the building in future.

An example of the constructive impact on the form of the building arising from the dialogue between the planning group and the architects is shown in the design development of the Science Reading Room. It was realized that the original proposal in the brief for three large low-ceilinged 'warehouse' floors would result in a claustrophobic mass of bookstacks without any sense of orientation. It was therefore decided to cut back the two upper floors to form a triple-height space along the axis of entry to allow the 'self-help' readers to find their way around; the working convenience of the readers was considered to be worth a certain loss of floor space.

Due respect for such significant differences in what the various departments of the Library really 'wanted to be' provided the evidence upon which their separate identity could be realized and celebrated. This recognition is the exact opposite of yesterday's 'Rationalism' that proposed a total absence of differentiation ostensibly in the interests of the catchphrase 'total flexibility' which, to permit any function to be located anywhere, resulted in a characterless 'non-place' in which no function can be served properly. Conversely real attention to marked differentiation in 'character' of the many elements of the building will manifest itself not only in detail but also in the disposition and massing of the whole building, as I hope to show.

It is by eliciting in this way the essential and different nature of patterns of use that each part of the building will be given its own form, character and therefore identity. Of the many advantages to be gained by giving such separate identity to each department of the buildng not the least is that the sheer size of the building is broken down to the scale of its working operations and therefore to the scale of the people using it.

The broad anatomy of the building that finally emerged from these studies took the form of two ranges of building. On the west the Humanities Reading Rooms ran north at a right-angle to Euston Road. On the east the Science Reading Rooms, straddling the administrative offices and conservation studios, diverged to run parallel to Midland Road. In the interspace between ran the main public concourse with access to Exhibition Galleries, Bookshop and Restaurant. In the south-east prow of the building, the Conference Centre enjoys its own separate identity.

So much for the basic horizontal distribution of elements. The vertical organization

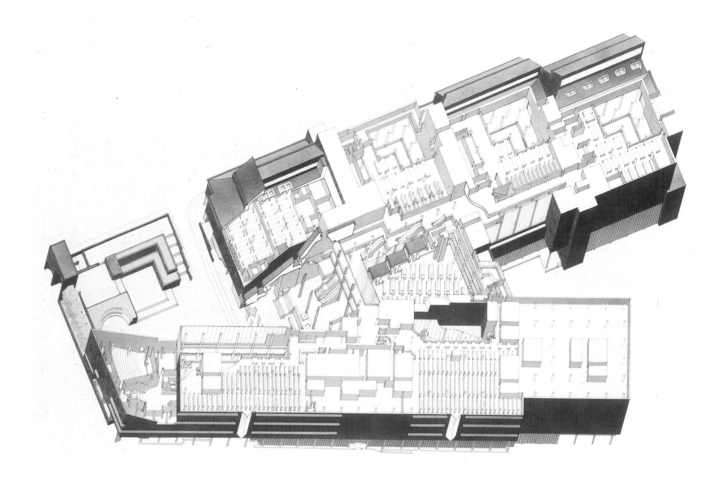

of the building was largely conditioned by the overriding importance that we attach to natural daylight as the ambient source of light wherever possible. Thus the reading rooms are located at the top under roof lanterns for natural daylight; the main areas for the general public (such as the Exhibition Galleries) at ground level: the mechanical plant for environmental services at first basement: and the rest of the basements dedicated to storage. The specific implications of these decisions are discussed in the description of these areas of the building below.

The resulting Brief acted not only as the original inspiration for design proposals but also, throughout the subsequent evolution of the scheme, as a critical grid against which response to changes could be measured whether they grew out of developments in technology, library services or political fiat.

The design process itself is a kind of alchemy which requires that, in the first place, the designer becomes immersed in the 'facts' derived from the Brief – dimensions, activities, inter-relationshps, priorities, numbers. The contradictions and conflicts of interest to which we have referred cannot be resolved by logic. The only way forward

Axonometric drawing of the original three-phase project (1975). Designed to be constructed in (self-sufficient) phases as funds became available. The western range (at the top of the image) houses the Humanities Reading Rooms, the eastern range houses the Sciences Reading Rooms. These straddle a central core of offices and laboratories with a further group of offices in the final phase. The Piazza on Euston Road is flanked by the Auditorium and Conference Centre. At this time the central concourse focused upon a conventional Catalogue Hall. (The Basement book-storage is not shown on this drawing.)

Diagrammatic model illustrating the vertical organization of the building. The top three floors contain the Reading Rooms with natural light introduced into the centre from above. Next the two-floor-high Exhibition Galleries are located at ground level with easy access for the general public. (Daylight is excluded for reasons of conservation.) First basement level is allocated to mechanical plant. The remaining basements house the storage of material largely, as here, in the form of mobile stacks. (Kandor Modelmakers. Coll: Sir Robert McAlpine Ltd)

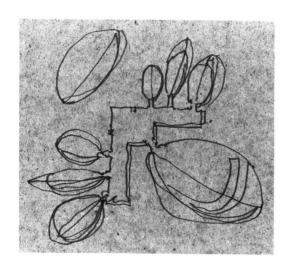

Typical design studies & ideograms.
British Museum Library (1962).
Relationship of Reading Rooms to
L-shaped Catalogue Hall likened to
ships moored to a dock.
(Drawing by Wilson)

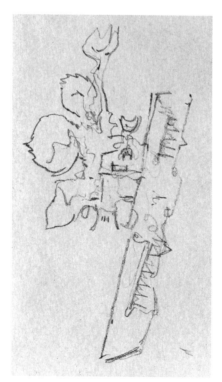

The British Library at St Pancras.
Irregular elements on left linked by
bridges over central concourse to
orthogonal spine on right.
(Drawing by Wilson)

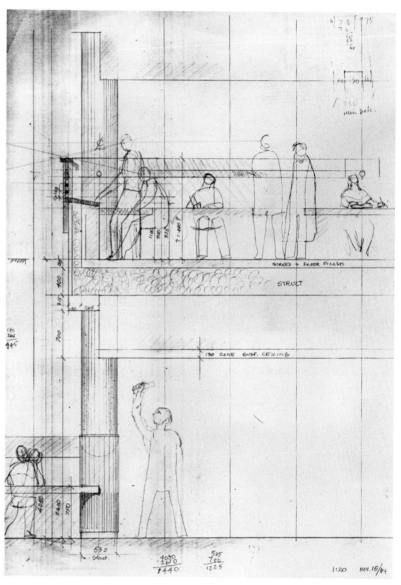

Typical study of working dimensions related to the human figure; Reading Room
balcony edge. (Drawing by Wilson)

Working model of Entrance Hall:
Colin St John Wilson at work.

is to make a comprehesive hypothesis – a design proposition – and then test it against the check-list of facts. The process is a kind of play, a search for the rules that will bring an appropriate order to the 'facts', rules of a game we might say that resolve those contradictions. And the first moves in the game take the form of innocent-looking ideograms, 'doodles', adumbrations.... What is imperative is that in the first place these studies contain a whole idea and secondly that this idea itself contains the seeds of its own subsequent development – into a building.

At the next stage the design proposals were fleshed out in models and drawings for review and, if necessary, revision. Last of all, prototype components were prepared for testing before final approval.

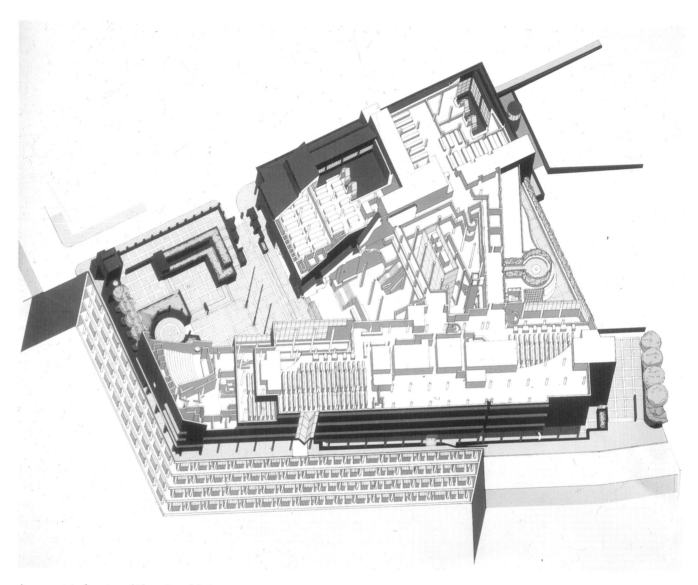

Axonometric drawing of Phase I modified to act as 'Completion Phase'. Note that the space
previously allocated to a Catalogue Hall now contains the King's Library and Public Restaurant.
The Readers and Friends' Common Room and Terrace is housed at roof level beyond.
The four floors of basement containing Mechanical Plant and Book Storage are shown in
diagrammatic form.

Growth and change

One overriding consideration grew out of the sheer size of the building as it emerged from the briefing process – 200,000 square metres. It became clear that it would not be possible, for financial reasons, to construct the building in a single contract. It would therefore be necessary to build the Library in phases as money became available. Furthermore it is of the essence of a Library to grow.

Accordingly a design for a scheme to be executed in three main phases was prepared. Clearly this could not be resolved by simply 'carving the joint into three portions'. The inevitable fact of extension in time would bring with it a period between the completion of one phase and commencement of the next whose length would always be an unknown factor so that a degree of self-sufficiency would have to be built in to each stage; secondly, allowance had to be made for the possibility of change in the nature of content and, consequently, of form.

As we have seen from Ruskin the freedom to deal with such variables is inherent in the ethos of the English Free School which, like T.S.Eliot's description of the English language, proudly boasts 'the greatest capacity for changing, and yet remaining itself'. An anatomy was therefore evolved that would provide a core building containing a basic minimum of each type of readership at the southern (Euston Road) end of the site, and would allow for the expansion northward in a consistent way – the Humanities on the western, and the Sciences on the eastern, flank of the site.

The size of the phasing increments was based upon the size of typical groupings of readers. Each stage was to be separated by vertical 'cores' providing lifts, stairs, mechanical and bookhandling services to each phase and these cores were also intended to act as a buffer for any one completed phase during the construction of the next.

In the event, Phase I of the original three-phase scheme was itself broken down into three further sub-stages of construction to match what can at best be called a cautious commitment to the furtherance of the project. In principle an open-endedness was what we had always intended. In practice, however, we never knew whether a further stage would be undertaken at all – let alone when it would be authorised. This uncertainty put to the test the capacity for adaptation in a severe way and meant that the Library administration had constantly to revise priorities for allocation of space in a frantic game of shrinkage, elimination and 'musical chairs' with the residue.

What has been built so far is Phase I only of the original scheme.

Symbolic form

Libraries are made of the stuff of myth. Somewhere within the silent miles of stacks, gallery upon gallery, and the associated web of information retrieval there awaits the discovery of those secret connections whose alchemy will at last combine to form the Philosopher's Stone: and it is a most compelling part of this myth that the discovery of this secret will one day be the achievement of a lone scholar: Faust, Einstein or....

And so to every scholar the library is a personal realm of secret topography and it is this perception that conditions the propriety of the public image of its architecture. It is no place for the rhetoric demanded by the grand celebrations of opera or theatre – for a library is not called upon to advertise the occasion that will draw a crowd of spectators to appointed times of performance. A comparison between the 'billboard' façade of the Paris Opéra inviting a huge audience and the single door leading into the walled courtyard of Labrouste's Bibliothèque Nationale makes the point. Timeless, massive and withdrawn, a library awaits the random arrival of its lonely explorers. Propriety that seeks a sensitive representation of this ambivalent character urges upon us a certain quietism of the kind described by Adolf Loos in which 'a building should be silent on the outside and reveal its wealth only on the inside'.

Nevertheless there is a sense in which a library has to be celebrated over and above the observance of duty: there is an inherent symbolic content that has to be given its embodiment and duly celebrated – something like the classical idea of a 'showing forth' of the inner significance of a place or an institution. At a time when there is no universally accepted language in which to celebrate such abstract ideas this is a delicate matter. Rhetoric, if it is to be intelligible, requires a public realm of shared values and beliefs. In writing about the absence of any such public realm in our time the poet W. H. Auden wryly observed that 'whenever a modern poet raises his voice he sounds phoney': Paul Verlaine had said more bluntly 'we have wrung the neck of rhetoric'. That architecture – a public art – should suffer the same inhibition is almost a contradiction in terms but it is, sadly, a predicament of our time. The attempt by the Post-modernists to overcome this fact by adopting formal conceits of the 18th century is as unconvincing as the opposite mode of abstract expressionism is disturbingly shrill. A future generation may find an authentic rhetoric: but we, where there is no common language to be shared, should proceed with caution.

What is important for any such celebration if it is to be free from phoney rhetoric is that it should be grounded in the facts of the case. In The British Library the symbolic role is most truly embodied in the King's Library. It was a condition of the gift to the nation of this great collection of George III that its beautiful leather and vellum bindings should be on show to the general public and not just to the scholars. The volumes have hitherto been distributed in the wall-cases of the British Museum where its identity, however handsome, has the passive character of decoration to the walls of the space dedicated to exhibitions. In the new building the collection is

The façade as advertisement and invitation to spectators: L'Opera Garnier, Paris (architect: Charles Garnier 1875).

The façade as protective screen: the central doorway leads into the courtyard of La Bibliothèque Nationale, Paris (architect Henri Labrouste. 1873).

housed in a free-standing structure, an object in its own right, a six-storey-high bronze and glass tower. By this transformation it becomes simultaneously a celebration of beautifully bound books, a towering gesture that announces the invisible presence of treasures housed below and a hard-working source of material studied in the Rare Book Reading Room opposite: the symbolic role is at one with the use.

This is an example of the way in which a library can be celebrated over and above the observance of duty. It recalls quite rightly the building Type used traditionally as a shrine and there is a certain analogy here to the famous Kaaba or 'Black Box' in Mecca.

There is also an issue of form raised by tendentious questions about planning for the future – devising a 'Library for the 21st century'. In dealing with this factor it has to be borne in mind that the occupancy of the greater part of the building is dedicated to purposes and practices of an unchanging nature – the storage and consultation of millions of items specifically to be preserved in their original form. To consult the Lindisfarne Gospels or the manuscript of 'Beowulf' the same basic conditions are required as those that were enjoyed when the work was first made. On the other hand it is inherent in the character of what is called 'cutting edge' technology that it is usually housed in short-life, rapidly replaced buildings, so that we tend to associate lightweight technology and deliberately transient 'styling' with the forefront of technological development.

It is inherent in the stylistic claims of 'high-tech' architecture that it must never look old, and obsolescence must be fought by constant replacement of out-of-date parts. However for the new national library it was specified that the building should have a working life of 200–250 years. In the event the building had to be so designed that changes to be accommodated were almost entirely electronic and therefore capable of replacement invisibly many times over in the life of the building. This has been done by forming continuous accessible voids at both ceiling and floor level throughout that which, for the most part, is an unchanging fabric.

A more appropriate poetic for such a building derives from the intention that running through the design there should be a sub-plot of metaphor and of allusions – either explicitly to historical precedent (as we have discussed in the case of the King's Library Tower) or to more recent precedent drawn from what has become, during this century, the very rich and diverse language of Modernism. Indeed it is very much in the nature of the Modernism to which I feel an allegiance (Eliot, Picasso, Stravinsky) that it is imbued with the historical sense of continuity and the practice of allusion rather than the clean slate of 'Modernismus' which denied all connection to the past.

(*opposite*) The King's Library, a six-floor tower of bronze and glass to display the leather and vellum bindings of George III's collection. (© Rhoden)

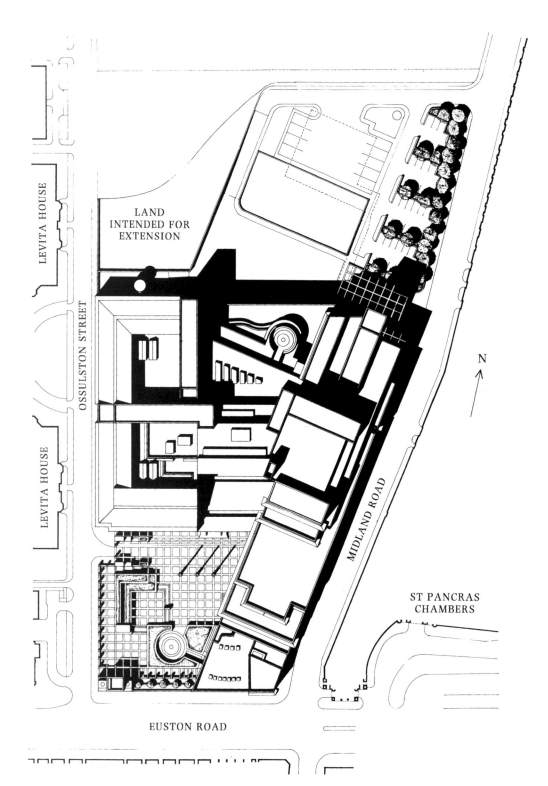

LEVITA HOUSE

LAND
INTENDED FOR
EXTENSION

OSSULSTON STREET

LEVITA HOUSE

N

MIDLAND ROAD

ST PANCRAS
CHAMBERS

EUSTON ROAD

Site Plan

Elements of the Building

The Site

Sited on the Euston Road between Euston Station to the west and St Pancras and King's Cross Stations to the east the location of The British Library is well served in terms of accessibility. Obviously the significance of this site will be greatly enhanced in the year 2002 if the enlargement of St Pancras Station to incorporate the main Terminal of the Cross-Channel Tunnel is carried out. The associated linkage to the Underground network and thereby to the other main-line railway stations in London would be equally advantageous.

Clearly there will be wide-ranging developments in the surrounding locality in response to the presence of the Library itself: booksellers, publishers and the international community of scholars as well as tourists will surely stimulate the flourishing of a new ambience of unique character, as the British Museum did in Bloomsbury. A whole new sector of London life is about to be generated.

The Library lies between two neighbouring buildings of architectural consequence. To the west the remarkable residential building, Levita House, was constructed in 1926–9 following a visit of the Building Committee of the Borough of St Pancras to the famous 'workers' fortresses' in Vienna of which the Karl Marx Hof by Karl Ehn is the most famous. Gentler by far than these imposing progenitors and sadly disrupted

The location of the Library alongside St Pancras (which may be developed northwards as the Terminal to the Cross-Channel Tunnel). King's Cross Station lies further to the east and Euston Station (out of picture) almost equidistant to the west.
(© Union Railways)

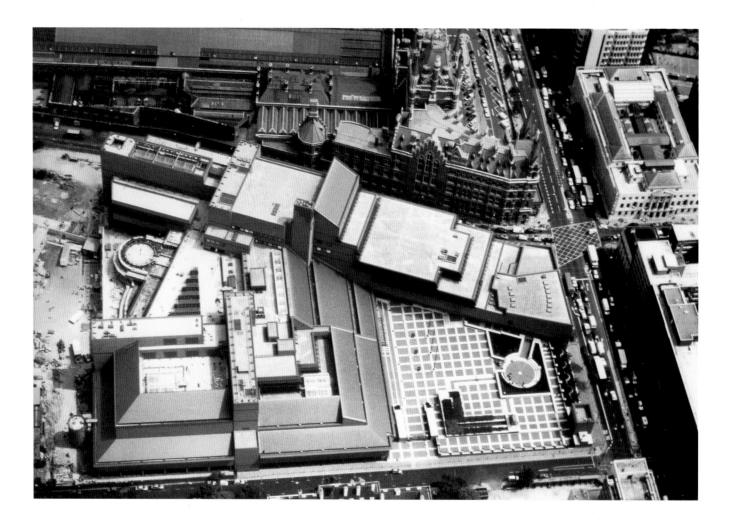

View of The British Library from the air. (© Sir Norman Foster).

in its original continuity of form by bomb-damage (would that it could be restored!) it still has a certain grandeur; with its courtyards and boldly arched pedestrian walkways it presents convenient points of linkage free from the traffic of Euston Road, to Chalcot Street which will surely generate a growing locale for second-hand bookshops, publishers' offices, cafés and pizzerias.

To the east stands St Pancras Chambers, one of London's great 'rogue' buildings with its towers, sheer walls of brick and huge slate roof, peppered with shafts of flues and dormer windows. Built in 1867 by George Gilbert Scott, it was the butt of ridicule by Pevsner as an archetypical example of the Victorian 'Battle of the Styles' so deplored by the Modernist orthodoxy. When the Library was relocated to this site in 1974 there were many who spoke of the need 'to get rid of that nonsense'. But there is a real sense in which, deeper than the borrowing of 'Gothic' idiom, there lies in this building a stirring of organic form that was the birth-mark of the great English Free School whose originality and significance we have discussed. The fact that the

Levita House, Ossulston Street. One of the archways and courtyards leading west into Chalcot Street, where future development in the manner of 'Bloomsbury' is predicted. (© Wilson)

St Pancras Chambers. A full-bodied, if rather ornate, example of the English Free School by Sir George Gilbert Scott (1876). (© Gascoigne)

equally great piece of engineering for the railway concourse itself (by W. H. Barlow and R. M. Ordish) was, in its day, the widest clear-span of covered space in the world should surely be an inspiration to the architect of any future development.

In placing the building on this site the different nature of these two neighbours helped to determine the particular location of parts of the Brief and the flexibility of organic form abetted the will to asymmetry of the internal organization to have its way and, in so doing, assert its true identity.

The southern (Euston Road) end was bound to remain the principal approach by train, by tube, by bus, and of course by foot from the University of London and the British Museum. It was clear, however, that the bulk of new building should be set back from this frontage principally in order to form an enclosed courtyard as protection from the hubbub of Euston Road but also thereby to preserve the stunning views of St Pancras Station approached from the west along Euston Road.

Strict constraints upon building height were laid down by the planning authority. These limitations conspired to confirm the decision on grounds of environmental stability to locate the very large storage areas below ground.

It was required that on Midland Road the large scale of the St Pancras shed should be mirrored by a building of equivalent height and mass whereas on the west (Ossulston Street) the right of each flat at ground level to good daylight had to be respected by working within the limiting profiles defined by the British Research Establishment daylight calculation system.

The Piazza

The main body of the Library itself is set back from Euston Road in order to allow for the creation of an enclosed courtyard to mediate between the turmoil of traffic on the main road and the point of entry into the building. The Piazza is further protected to the east from the heavy traffic on Midland Road by the projection of the Science Reading Room and Conference Centre southwards to Euston Road.

There are a number of entrances of which the principal one is through the Portico sited in the south-west corner. A secondary entrance at the south-east corner passes diagonally under the Conference Centre from the point where, 'sotto-portico', it houses a small snack-bar. The axes of these two points of entry intersect at the location of a major sculptural monument – the bronze figure of Newton (after William Blake) by Sir Eduardo Paolozzi. Behind it and down the complete length of the western flank an upper terrace offers the possibility of hosting such activities as second-hand book stalls, open-air celebrations or fairs. Steps and a ramp lead down to the main (lower) level of the Piazza in which a small amphitheatre (to which is promised a ring of granite sculptures by Anthony Gormley) forms the focus for other planned open-air events. A variety of 'places' is provided for meeting or simply for private relaxation in good weather.

The Conference Centre has its own independent entrance in the Piazza itself but

(on opposite page)

Piazza and Portico; an early study by Wilson.

The British Library Portico. The lettering in red sandstone was cut by the Cardozo Kindersley Workshop, as also the design in letters of the bronze-cast gates. (© Charles)

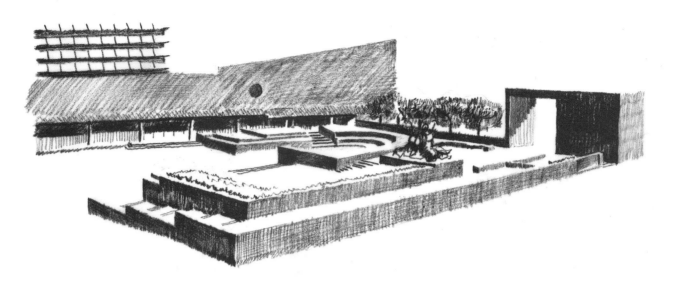

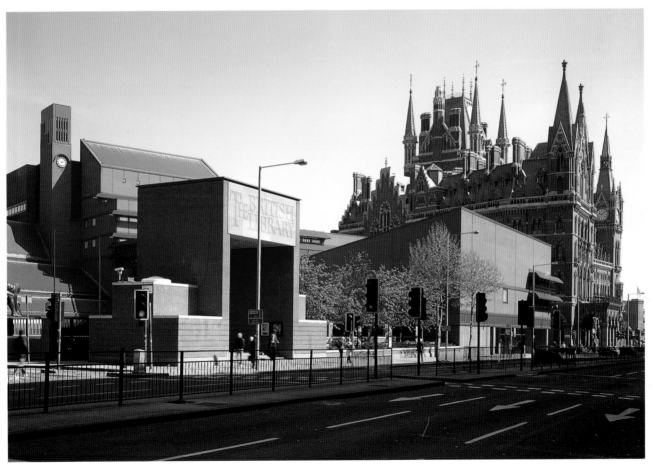

View through the portico gates across the piazza to the main entrance. (© Donat)

The Piazza viewed from the Portico. The Newton monument by Eduardo Paolozzi on the left and St Pancras Chambers on the right overlooking the Sciences Reading room and Conference Centre. (© Mainstream)

this can also be reached under cover by the third entrance point to the Library which leads from Midland Road.

The entrance to the Library itself lies in the north-east corner of the courtyard flanked to the left by the display window of the Bookshop.

The general form of the building is a direct reflection of the volumetric content within and, in being so, embodies the fundamental asymmetry in the pattern of use in the reading rooms to which we have alluded. Thus the western range of the building houses the closed-access Humanities reading rooms and therefore receives its daylight through rooflights and clerestories and has no windows whereas the eastern range, which houses the open-access reading rooms of the Science Collections, derives its daylight from side windows continuous with horizontal louvres. The roof of the central entrance and concourse rises in a catenary of three steepening waves. The tower containing various service shafts assumes in addition the status of a formal clock-tower.

The primary purpose of the Piazza enclosure is that it will allow the visiting reader to regain the tranquillity that was lost in the street and also to have a place in good weather in which to rest between spells of work. It is however also open in normal day-time hours to the general public: and since it is the only open public space in the neighbourhood and, furthermore, will lie adjacent to the proposed Channel Tunnel

Terminal, it should take on the unique sense of a place of a rendez-vous not only for the Library but also to visitors to and from the Continent.

The big roof is both the most direct solution as well as the clearest indication of the presence of large spatial volumes within. In so being it not only helps to relate the Library to the roofs of St Pancras Chambers compositionally but also, by reference to many historic precedents, underlines the monumental status of the Library itself.

Brick was chosen as the facing material both because it is the one material that in this climate improves rather than degenerates in appearance over time but also to orchestrate the Library on a broad scale with St Pancras whose bricks come from the same source in Leicestershire. The colours for the metal sun louvres and trim to the ground floor panels and columns were also selected as common to both buildings.

The upper portion of the Science Reading Room was cut back to allow more of St Pancras Chambers to be seen from the Piazza, the inimitable ornateness of the hotel being deliberately complemented by a certain austerity in the Library itself.

Detail of the
Midland Road
façade.
(© Charles)

(*opposite*) View towards the
entrance doors from the
'amphitheatre' in the Piazza.
(© Donat)

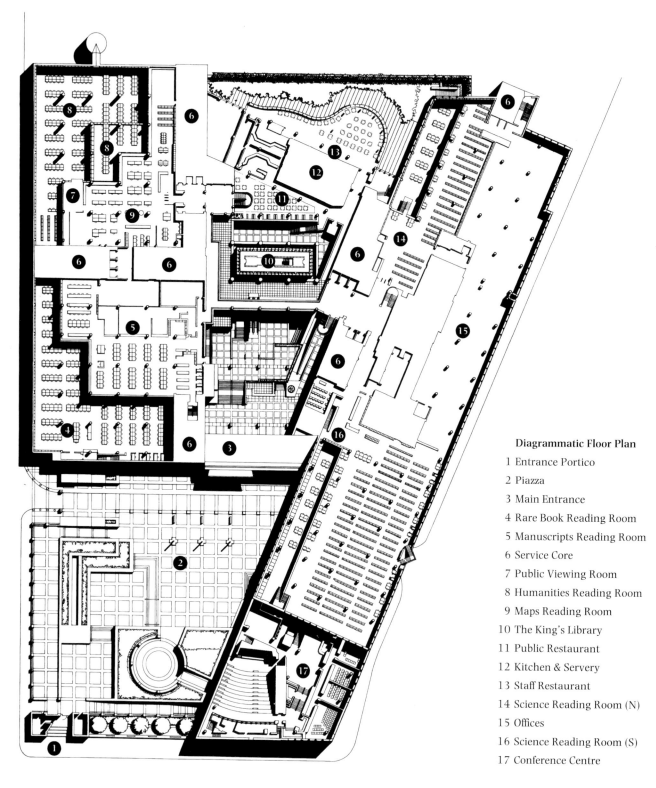

Diagrammatic Floor Plan

1 Entrance Portico

2 Piazza

3 Main Entrance

4 Rare Book Reading Room

5 Manuscripts Reading Room

6 Service Core

7 Public Viewing Room

8 Humanities Reading Room

9 Maps Reading Room

10 The King's Library

11 Public Restaurant

12 Kitchen & Servery

13 Staff Restaurant

14 Science Reading Room (N)

15 Offices

16 Science Reading Room (S)

17 Conference Centre

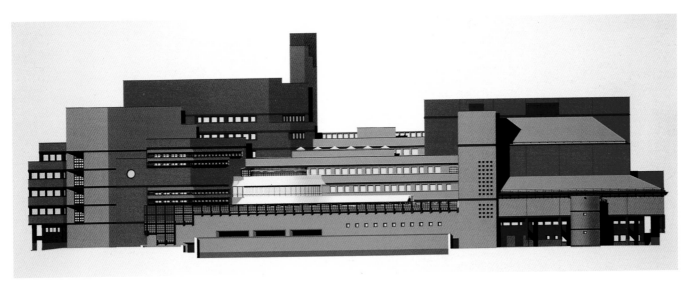

(*above, top*) South façade (*above*) North façade. Silkscreen prints (Wilson).

The Main Entrance Hall

The Main Entrance Hall to the Library takes the form of a generous concourse affording not only access to the reading rooms for scholars and students but also for members of the general public to visit the Exhibition Galleries, the Bookshop and Centre for the Book and school parties visiting the Education Service.

First, we have tried to abide by the adage 'one should not have to ask the way in a public building'. On entering, the visitor can instantly see the general distribution of elements in the building and the route or point of entry to all the main destinations; and as one moves around the building there are, here and there, a number of port-hole windows offering orientation views to the individual visiting the Library for the first time.

The Library is a large building and the architectural strategy has above all been to make of the entrance a place of invitation rather than a presence whose sheer size would seem to threaten the visitor. To this end the scale is modulated gently in progressive increments of size starting with a ceiling that is low at the threshold but ascends in a sequence of waves to the full height at the centre five and a half floors above entrance level.

Secondly the predominant light source is natural daylight, pouring in through clerestory and rooflights, reflecting off the light coloured floor and permitting

Main Entrance Hall.
A view from the point of entry
(© Donat)

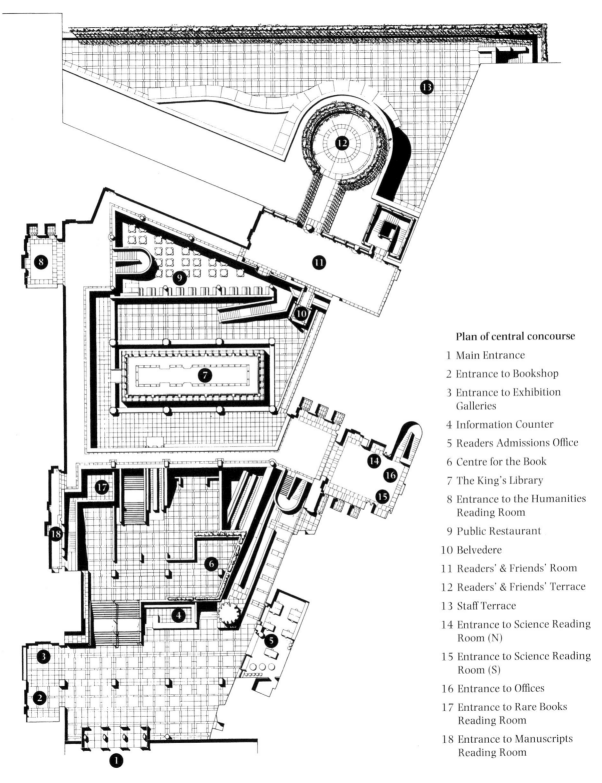

Plan of central concourse

1 Main Entrance

2 Entrance to Bookshop

3 Entrance to Exhibition
  Galleries

4 Information Counter

5 Readers Admissions Office

6 Centre for the Book

7 The King's Library

8 Entrance to the Humanities
  Reading Room

9 Public Restaurant

10 Belvedere

11 Readers' & Friends' Room

12 Readers' & Friends' Terrace

13 Staff Terrace

14 Entrance to Science Reading
   Room (N)

15 Entrance to Science Reading
   Room (S)

16 Entrance to Offices

17 Entrance to Rare Books
   Reading Room

18 Entrance to Manuscripts
   Reading Room

(*top*) North-south sectional model of central concourse. Entrance doors on the left, the King's Library in the middle, public and staff restaurants and terraces on the right. (Kandor Modelmakers)

(*above, left*) A 'porthole' view into the concourse looking west. (© Donat)

(*above,right*) A 'porthole' view into the concourse looking east. (© Donat)

(*opposite*) On the left the figure of Shakespeare by Roubiliac; in the centre the tapestry based on R.B. Kitaj's painting 'If not, not' and made by the Edinburgh Weavers: on the right, four busts in roundels of donors to the Collections. (© Donat)

Main Entrance Hall.
A view from East Staircase
(© Donat)

Main Entrance Hall.
A view towards East Staircase
(© Donat)

occasional shafts of sunlight to glance down the wall surfaces. As a result the passage of entry from the Piazza is a gentle transition into an 'in-between' space whose duality between inside and out is further underlined by the continuity into the interior of the wall and pavement finishes of the Piazza.

Thirdly the sheer size of the concourse is broken down to human scale by threading throughout the space an intermediary set of elements. For example the two bridges that connect the east and west ranges of reading rooms assert the 'normal' dimension of floor height. In the same way the canopies, carved seats and balustrades and the clusters of suspended lights assert a human scale much as street-furniture (lamp-post, railing & pedestrian crossing) moderate and mediate between traffic and people. Above all bodily assurance draws upon a sense of mass.

Natural materials with self-finish have been chosen not only in order to reduce the level of maintenance but above all for their sensuous response to touch – travertine, oak, leather, brass and ebony.

Carved travertine stone for seat and balustrade.
(© Donat)

Staircase handrail combining polished brass and bound leather.
(© Wilson)

Door handle combining polished brass and bound leather.
(© Donat)

The nature of the building as a library is celebrated by the siting of a number of memorial busts and appropriate works of art. First the figure of Shakespeare (a copy of the sculpture by Roubiliac) stands on a high plinth close to the entrance doors. Next the huge tapestry based on R. B. Kitaj's narrative painting 'If not, not' hangs on the adjacent wall; beyond it four roundels carry the head and shoulder busts of major donors to the collections – Grenville, Banks, Cotton and Sloane.

Most powerful of all, the bronze and glass tower housing the King's Library, which we have already described in terms of its symbolic role, soars up in all its splendour of leather and vellum bindings from the basement below to rise six-floors high as the symbolic centre of the whole building; the suggestion of its origin in the deep book basements below is emphasized by the use of polished black marble around its base whose reflections convey, by 'trompe l'oeuil', the impression of receding into limitless depth. By this means the architecture has been able to signal to the visitor in the Main Entrance Hall the existence of the huge underworld of stored treasures.

Beyond the King's Library there rises a small lift-shaft tower crowned by a 'belvedere' which commands a view across the whole 'city scape' of the concourse all the way back to the entrance doors.

The King's Library on the left; the public restaurant on the right. (© Donat)

(*opposite*) On the right the King's Library (before installation of the books); in the centre, the 'belvedere' tower and, below, the coffee-bar; on the left the public restaurant. (© Donat)

General Amenity

There are a number of places dedicated specifically to the amenity of readers, the general public and the staff.

Roof terrace for Friends of the Library and Readers. (© Donat)

To enable parties of visitors to see into the large Humanities Reading Room without causing any disturbance to readers the design included a route of access by lift from the Treasures Gallery to a viewing gallery at third floor level: from this vantage point a full view of the Humanities Reading Room can be enjoyed.

We have already described the main features of the entrance Piazza. In order to provide a source of refreshment to people in it a coffee / snack bar has been incorporated in the south-east corner 'sotto-portico' beneath the Conference Centre. Within the concourse of the Main Entrance Hall a self-service restaurant for both readers and general public is located beyond the King's Library. There is also a café area at the level below, open to all. In both cases the predominant view is, very appropriately, towards the beautiful bindings on show in the glass tower.

On the third floor Readers and Friends of the Library share separate areas of a

The staff restaurant
(© Donat)

common-room which, on the Main Entrance Hall side, has access to the 'belvedere' with views right back to the entrance doors and, to the north, access to a roof-terrace with splendid views to Hampstead. The terrace is circular in form, enveloped by a metal and timber lattice to support climbing plants. This screen is punctured at seven points by low column bases to receive sculpture. It is a high place of rest and contemplation, enclosed but open to the sky.

Finally there is a restaurant for staff overlooked by recreation and common rooms and opening out into a large screened terrace. This room will also be used occasionally for entertainment and celebration.

In the north-facing elevation this whole zone of amenity is seen to lie between the diverging east and west ranges of the building which extend in widening arms to embrace it. The lattice screens ensure both security and a certain desirable privacy which would still be retained if further extension to the north is made.

Courtyard of the staff restaurant. (© Wilson)

(*opposite*) North face of the staff terrace with the Readers' and Friends' roof terrace above. (© Donat)

The Reading Rooms

In the Library there are eleven reading areas which are broadly divided into the two very different patterns of use, which in our description of the development of the Brief we defined in terms of open- and closed-access to material.

Thus, in the closed-access reading rooms assigned to the Humanities Collections (which occupy the western range of the building) the space is almost entirely occupied by readers at their desks. Reference material lines the walls but for the most part the books that are consulted are drawn from the storage basements.

There is a wide range of reading rooms of this type, varying in size and each with its own quite specific character. The largest is three floors high with stepped terraces like a hanging-garden. Here the top-most level is the Maps Reading Room where the size and nature of the material to be studied required display tables very different from the general reading desks. Next in size, the Rare Book Reading Room is overlooked

Middle level of the Humanities Reading Room. (© Durant)

(*opposite*)
The Humanities Reading Room, showing all three levels of which the top 'terrace' is the Maps Reading Room. The space is naturally lit in the centre from clerestory and roof lanterns. (© Donat)

by the Manuscripts Reading Room. In the Reading Room for the Oriental and India Office Collections it is proposed that a number of the magnificent paintings in the collection should be hung high on the wall over the open-access stacks.

Most of the readers in these rooms are committed to an extended period of research so that the Reading Room becomes a long-term place of work. The prime consideration here has therefore been to create a working ambience for sustained occupation and study. To this end the employment of daylight as the primary source of ambient light is given priority and it is poured into the centre of the space by means of clerestory and lantern lights housed in the pitched roofs.

Conversely in the eastern range of the building the Science and Patents Collections in the form of abstracts, periodicals and books less than thirty years old are disposed on 'open-access' shelves which occupy the greater part of the floor space and to which readers are invited to help themselves.

Since the centre of the space is fully occupied by the bookshelves, daylight is introduced from the side through windows to reader positions which are accordingly

The Reading Room for the
Oriental & India Office Collections.
(Drawing by Wilson)

(*opposite*) Humanities Reading Room
(© Freeman)

The South Sciences Reading
Room, showing the triple-height
reading area. (© Donat)

The South Sciences Reading Room second floor. (© Donat)

located along both perimeters – the Midland Road frontage on the east and the balcony edge on the west. A three-floor-high shaft of space is opened up along the axis of entry to the Reading Room to enable the readers to orientate themselves in their searches throughout the space.

In all cases material may be summoned from the storage basements through the computerized catalogue, request and delivery systems.

Each reader has a range of generously dimensioned desks (of which the smallest is 1.140 m wide and 750 mm deep) made of oak with leather-top surface, and served with individual light source and power outlets for computer, microreader or other equipment: a warning light informs the reader of the arrival at the control desk of books requested. A specially designed chair and, if required, footstool complete the specification of 'workplace' for every reader. There are also a number of closed 'carrels' for single or shared occupation distributed within each reading room.

These and other such facilities have enormously increased the reader's powers of search and substantially improved the delivery time of material on request. But the major architectural question still remains as it always has – how do you create the ambience for sustained study in a room occupied by 300–500 individual readers?

To an architect the most haunting image of the solitary scholar is the painting of St Jerome (the patron saint of scholars) by Antonello da Messina which hangs in the National Gallery, London. Ensconced in a timber shell raised four steps above the cold tiled floor, the scholar is enveloped in a purpose-made aedicule of bookshelf, ledge and desk like an organist's console. The whole structure forms a frame of attention focused upon the act of reading: and in its turn this delicate barque is enveloped within a high-vaulted structure of stone. It is the very embodiment of intense silent concentration in a hierarchy of space and a palette of materials each of which responds to purpose by its scale, position, texture and orientation to light for this fortunate scholar.

But huge contradictions enter into play where it is a case of serving not one but a thousand readers, particularly since each one of the thousand still claims the right to that privileged aura. Here the crux of the matter lies in the manipulation of scale by

'St. Jerome' by Antonello da Messina (National Gallery, London).

(*opposite*) Reader consulting catalogue on middle floor of Humanities Reading Room. (© Donat)

The Rare Book & Music Reading Room, with the Manuscripts Reading Room at the balcony level above. (© Donat)

Humanities Reading Room seen from Visitor's Room at Level 3. (© Donat)

the creation and sustaining of elements that bridge the difference between what serves the individual (chair, table, footstool . . .) and what serves 'the others' (enfilades of reader-tables, light-fittings, book trolleys, information desks, catalogue search points). Provision for easy circulation must be channelled to avoid invasiveness and balcony edges are given such depth that a reader above cannot peer over and distract or 'threaten' a reader below. Noisy consultation areas and issue desks are concentrated in single height areas where noise can be largely absorbed with acoustic ceilings. The large study areas with high ceilings and long views are generally quiet with carpeted floors and sound-absorbent perforations in the ceiling vaults.

Guides to the lighting of libraries call for consistently high levels of illumination and relatively even light levels to avoid glare. Important though it is, this advice covers only part of the lighting task. Light levels which are too uniform can produce a directionless, almost underwater environment, as fatiguing in its own way as the irritation caused by glare.

The lighting strategy in the British Library is closely tied to its spatial strategy. In the single-height areas which are either used for offices (with views out) or open-access stack, the direct fluorescent lights are regularly spaced to allow easy adaptability from the one use to another. In the larger reading rooms, the long views, so important for mental alertness, are not provided by views through windows, but by views across large rooms. The quality of these internal 'landscapes' is largely determined by the quality of light, both natural and artificial, albeit that priority is given wherever possible to natural light.

Daylight is introduced as the principal source of ambient light; its properties of vividness and variation are a source of stimulation that no artificial lighting system can emulate and they bring to the reader the further stimulus of an awareness of the natural rhythms of the day and season – the passage of the sun and shifts in the weather – a rewarding relief from sustained concentration on a close task. It is introduced at high level, and sunbeams are even permitted to hit sloped ceiling surfaces, giving the room the quality of a bright shaded clearing in a forest. The artificial light accentuates those qualities – the ceiling surfaces are washed with indirect (low energy) light, giving a gentle background light equally comfortable to the reader using a monitor or taking notes. But direct light picks out the spines of the books in the surrounding shelves, the service and information counters, and the main circulation routes.

At each desk, a switchable desk light allows the reader to select ideal conditions for screen reading (light off) or for book reading and establishes a local focus of attention, the printed page being, as it should, the brightest surface in the field of vision. Even in distribution to prevent glare, the light levels are varied enough to provide an endlessly interesting, dappled landscape, shifting and breathing as clouds pass overhead.

Finally there is the difficult-to-define but ever present 'body-language' that in every one of us engages in a deeply personal sensitivity to varying degrees of spatial envelopment or exposure. Thus the location and spatial disposition of each desk is intentionally very varied. For instance in the Humanities Reading Room the difference between a reader's table at the balcony edge or one that is 'tucked in' below the terrace above or one that lies in the tall perimeter vault offers a generous choice to the reader and in all cases opens up a long-range view across the room as stimulating contrast to the concentrated focus of close study upon page and monitor.

The old Round Reading Room offered one all-embracing spatial gesture to the reader. It had its splendour but if offered no choice of shelter to those who found it a little relentless in its exposure. Here there is a quite unique variety in the range of choice for location, form and dispositon of workplace and as a further consequence of this design approach each of the eleven reading rooms has an inherently different identity of its own.

Natural light from the clerestory
window in the upper vault of
the Humanities Reading Room.
(© Wilson)

The 'John Ritblat Gallery: Treasures of The British Library'. (© Charles)

Exhibition Galleries

The Library's collection of manuscripts, rare books, music and maps is unequalled in the world and its proper display to the general public plays a major part in the life of the building. To this end a shared foyer, accessible directly from the main Entrance Hall, gives access to three Galleries.

The 'John Ritblat Gallery: Treasures of The British Library' displays precious items from the permanent collections – music, sacred texts, illuminated manuscripts, incunabula, maps and globes, with set-piece displays for certain key documents such as Magna Carta and the Lindisfarne Gospels. The 'Pearson Gallery of Living Words at The British Library' houses several themed exhibitions based on material drawn from the Library's own collections replaced from time to time by large-scale temporary exhibitions. A third Gallery ('The Workshop') dedicated to the history of communications houses displays of a more explicitly didactic nature combining both traditional and interactive forms of presentation.

All of these Galleries are open to all-comers and play a major role in the educational services offered by the Library.

The character of these spaces is determined by the low light-level that is required for the conservation of works on paper. As a consequence it is the one public space in which daylight is excluded altogether. The intended ambience is therefore of a low-lit cavern in which the treasures of the collection are displayed in showcases lit from within by small fibre-optic lenses. In this way heat and the ultra-violet rays that are so damaging to such material are removed from the point of display. In appearance however these small light-points give a sparkling jewel-like appearance that is entirely consistent with the size and exquisite nature of much of the material which is displayed.

(*opposite*) On the left the staircase down to the 'Temporary Exhibitions Gallery': on the right the staircase up to the 'Treasures Gallery'. (© Charles)

The Conference Centre. 'The Spanish Steps'. (© Rhoden)

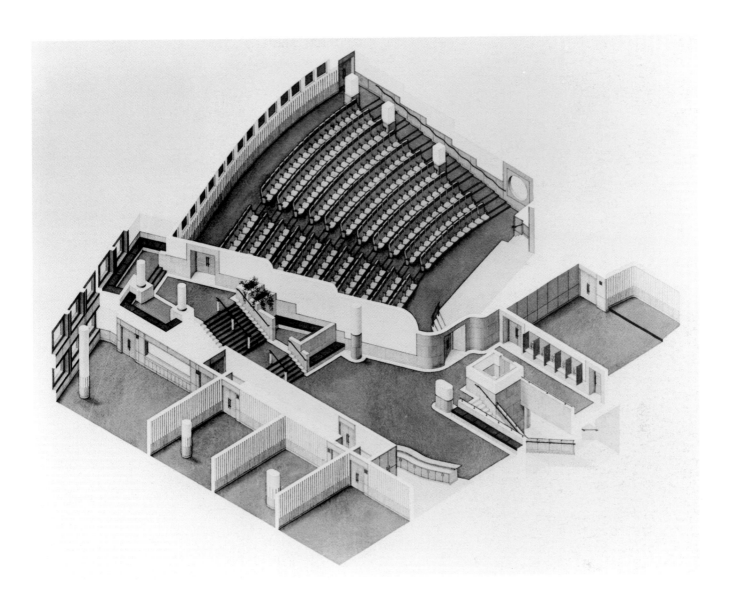

Axonometric of Conference Centre showing the Auditorium with associated seminar rooms served by the bar, foyer and 'Spanish Steps' seating area. (Drawing by Dennis Dornan)

Conference Centre

The eastern flank of the Piazza is enclosed by a Conference Centre. This has its own entrance and therefore enjoys complete independence from the Library itself with respect to access and programme activities.

Its principal purpose originally was to create a base for conferences and lectures in the field of library scholarship or any other appropriate themes together with the inhouse training and educational activities of the Library. In the course of construction some design modification has been introduced to allow for a limited level of use for external conferences. The accommodation includes an Auditorium to seat

The Conference Centre. The main Auditorium (250 seats). Projection and simultaneous translation booths at rear: 'porthole' view to Piazza. (© Donat)

The Conference Centre. A seminar room. (© Durant)

250 with facilities for simultaneous translation, film, sound and video presentations;
four seminar rooms ranging in capacity between 20–65 seats each and a large foyer
and bar with provision for catering services.

Here again, all of these rooms, including the Auditorium, can be daylit – although
all have provision for blackout. Lectures and seminars entail long periods
of sedentary attendance and, as in the reading rooms, daylight is seen to be both a
stimulant to attention and a saving grace against moments of tedium.

The foyer to the bar contains a broad staircase with seating nooks to left and
right as suitable places for refreshment and discussion during intervals. The casual
encounter is an essential extension to conference activities and, by analogy with the
'Spanish Steps' in Rome, the architecture here seeks to create the appropriate relaxed
ambience and sense of place to encourage such random contacts.

Staff areas

I have described above the need for certain areas of the building to have the property
of flexibility that will allow them to serve equally well for bookstacks, reader spaces or
offices. Such provision is principally located in the eastern building range facing
Midland Road: and it is in the centre of that block that the staff entrance is located.

Office planning. A study model (with
collaged figures) to demonstrate the
relation of the work-station furthest
from a window to views out of the
building. (Wilson)

Office at Upper Ground Level.
(© Donat)

On this basis the operational and environmental parameters for the design of office space were the subject of close investigation and led to the drawing up of their own intrinsic family of rules and priorities. One of the first of these was that even in the deepest plan of layout every workplace commanded an uninterrupted view out of a window. The appropriate working dimensions, furniture and equipment for particular tasks and desirable characteristics for workstations were established: these included the pattern of distribution of power outlets to workstations, location of partitions and storage units in relation to ceiling lighting, escape routes, and the minimising of disruption at times of window cleaning.

Within these rules the optimum location of groups of offices could be determined whether it be enclosed in the territory of a particular Department or made easily accessible to visitors or, as in the case of Studios and Conservation Laboratories, located on the top floor to ensure optimum conditions for daylight (e.g. for colour matching and detail).

The Board Room. The chairs and table were designed by Ron Carter. (© Donat)

Storage, conservation and distribution

The greater part of the 340 linear kilometres of shelving for books, manuscripts, maps and other collections is stored in three and a half floors below ground. This is for two reasons.

The most stable environmental conditions, free from variation in local or seasonal changes in weather, can be secured below ground. It follows that this steady-state enables the maintenance of constant environmental conditions with the minimum expenditure of energy. (Temperature $17°C \pm 1$; humidity $50\% \pm 5\%$).

Books are stored either in conventional fixed stacks or in mobile shelving. It necessarily follows that there is a wide range of other forms of shelf and cabinet types and dimensions to receive maps, manuscripts and unique incunabula. The floor structure is designed throughout to accommodate the very considerable loading imposed by mobile shelving. (14 kilonewtons per m^2)

When it came to the selection of a system for delivering books the choice was not, perhaps, an obvious one at first glance. There were on the market a number of new and very streamlined document-conveying systems. However, all but the 'old fashioned' systems were produced by one firm only, whereas belt and paternoster

Basement book storage. A row of manually operated mobile bookstacks. (© Rhoden)

Book-tray being dispatched from basement sorting area. (© Rhoden)

elevator technology was available from several sources capable of putting together a combination of rollers, electric motors, chains, and a steel framework. In case of the failure of one manufacturer, such a system could be sustained by another. (The Bodleian Library in Oxford is still using the paternoster elevator which was installed in the 1930s.) The relatively slow operating speed of such systems is not a drawback in this case – bookbindings are not best preserved by subjecting them to rapid acceleration and deceleration.

It is convenient at the uppermost level of the basement to dedicate a continuous horizontal layer to a system for the delivery and return of books. The stored books can be delivered from all basements to any above-ground location without requiring any horizontal routes in the superstructure itself (which would have been both space-consuming and insecure). The system devised for this purpose is generated from control despatch points in a number of discrete compartments. At each of these points requests for items are received and the item itself retrieved by hand. It is then put into

BOOK DELIVERY SYSTEM
IN THE COMPLETED SCHEME

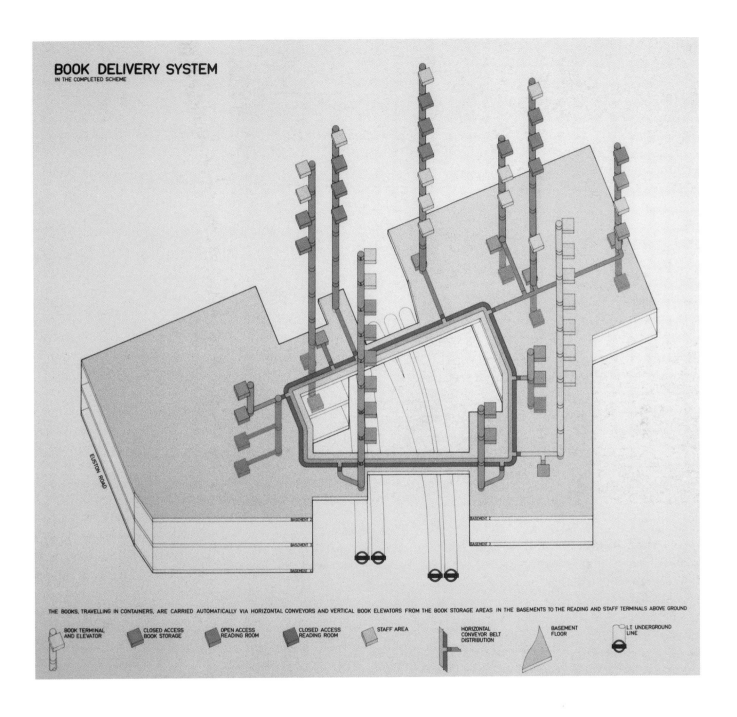

EUSTON ROAD

BASEMENT 2

BASEMENT 3

BASEMENT 4

BASEMENT 1

BASEMENT 2

BASEMENT 3

THE BOOKS, TRAVELLING IN CONTAINERS, ARE CARRIED AUTOMATICALLY VIA HORIZONTAL CONVEYORS AND VERTICAL BOOK ELEVATORS FROM THE BOOK STORAGE AREAS IN THE BASEMENTS TO THE READING AND STAFF TERMINALS ABOVE GROUND

BOOK TERMINAL AND ELEVATOR

CLOSED ACCESS BOOK STORAGE

OPEN ACCESS READING ROOM

CLOSED ACCESS READING ROOM

STAFF AREA

HORIZONTAL CONVEYOR BELT DISTRIBUTION

BASEMENT FLOOR

L.T. UNDERGROUND LINE

Mechanical book-delivery system. Horizontal travellators serve vertical paternoster lifts to service counters in reading rooms, conservation laboratories, cataloguing offices, etc. (Wilson)

a plastic container tray whose bar-code is matched with the destination code by light-pen. The tray will then be carried on horizontal conveyors and thence into paternoster elevators to the control room serving the point of request. Return to storage is achieved by reversing the procedure.

This automated request, retrieval and delivery system ensures that required items can arrive within thirty minutes to the point of request. Where the material is either too fragile or too large to fit into the containers it must be conveyed by hand.

The building was accordingly designed around horizontal and vertical paths by means of conveyor belts and paternoster elevators. The computer-run coding and code-reading system allows any container to be sent directly to any of the terminals in the building. This electronic control system is a 'bolt-on' which can easily be modified as technology advances. In fact, during the installation of the system, modifications were made to the control equipment because improved versions had come on the market.

Works of art

It had been the intention, right from the start, to include works of art in the design of the building – not just to add them later as decoration but to incorporate them into the architecture, embodying and elaborating upon the many themes addressed by a library and thereby helping to establish the special identity of the building. This entailed the selection of strategic locations for works already in the possession of the Library and the commissioning of new works.

The first two major commissions were for a large tapestry in the Main Entrance Hall and a focal monument in the Piazza. In each case the work chosen was by an artist renowned for a concern with subject-matter – literary, mythical or historical, as indeed befits a library.

The choice of artist for the tapestry fell upon R.B. Kitaj whose great contribution to the art of our day has been to re-introduce subject matter into painting when abstraction was all the cry. He once declared that 'books are to me what trees are to a landscape painter' and he has been called 'the history painter of our time'. His painting 'If not, not' draws upon themes both in literature (Conrad's *Heart of Darkness* and T. S. Eliot's *The Waste Land*) and in painting (Giorgione's '*La Tempesta*' and a landscape by Bassano) – food for thought as well as a field of glowing colour. The tapestry is the largest single-loom tapestry ever to be made in this country (7 metres by 7 metres) and was carried out by the Edinburgh Weavers through a joint sponsorship of the Arts Council and private gifts donated to the memory of the Marquess of Bute. It hangs upon the left-hand wall of the Main Entrance Hall.

The monumental bronze figure of Newton by Sir Eduardo Paolozzi also, like the tapestry, carries allusions of a poetic and philosophical nature. While it recalls the famous painting by William Blake its superb Michelangelesque figure is nevertheless crossed by ironic allusions to robots and artificial intelligence which reflect Blake's

(*opposite*) Newton monument by Sir Eduardo Paolozzi. The sculpture is located at the point of intersection of the two axes of entrance from Euston Road – one at the south-eastern corner and the other, shown here, at the Portico. The image refers to the painting of Newton by William Blake. (© Donat)

Bust of Sir Hans Sloane, whose huge collection of books and manuscripts came to the British Museum at its foundation in 1753 and is now a constituent part of the Library's collections. The bust is mounted in a roundel in the Main Entrance Hall. Copy made by Leo Stevenson. (© Rhoden)

own reservations about the ambition of the scientist (as he saw it) to reduce everything to the measurable. This work is the gift of the Foundation for Sport & Art and as the first such gift to the Library at a time when all Government funding for works of art had been withdrawn it stands as a gesture of outstanding significance as well as generosity.

The figure creates a powerful brooding presence at the point of intersection of the two axes of entry to the site from Euston Road.

In the Piazza amphitheatre eight stone colonnettes rise from the back of the encircling seats to carry large boulders of ancient Aberdeen granite incised by the sculptor Anthony Gormley with primitive images of the human body. This work, which was the winning submission in a competition, juxtaposes in a very poetic way the mechanistic overtones of Paolozzi's Newton with allusions to the first images made by man in Palaeolithic caverns.

The bronze gates to the Portico itself were the work of David Kindersley (at one time an assistant in the workshop of Eric Gill) and his wife Lida Cardozo, who together also executed the carving in sandstone over the Portico itself.

There are a number of works already owned by the Library prominently displayed in the Entrance Hall. On a raised plinth immediately in front of the entrance doors stands the copy of the figure of Shakespeare by Roubiliac and, on the wall beyond the tapestry, a group of four roundels containing copies of the portrait busts of donors and founders of the Library Collections – Sir Hans Sloane by Rysbrack, Sir Robert Cotton by Roubiliac, Thomas Grenville attributed to Nollekens, Sir Joseph Banks by Damer.

In the ante-room to the Rare Book & Music Reading Room herms carry busts of Handel by Roubiliac, Vaughan Williams by David McFall (1957), Virginia Woolf by Stephen Tomlin (1935) and T. S. Eliot by Celia Scott (1997), and portrait paintings of Bach by Elias Haussmann and Charles Lamb by H. Meyer; and at the entrance of the main Humanities Reading Room a bust celebrates the memory of the great Librarian of the British Museum Library and creator of the old Round Reading Room, Sir Anthony Panizzi by Carlo Marochetti.

Many paintings and busts from the rich collection of works inherited from the India Office Library are distributed throughout the building – notably in the Oriental and India Office Collections Reading Room and the Board Room. Works of sculpture by Dhruva Mistry and William Woodrow have been donated to the Library and other important works by contemporary artists have been the subject of donation or acquisition. In the field of graphics, most notable of these are a set of etchings by Frank Auerbach, photographs by Fay Godwin and the screenprints based on famous book-covers by R. B. Kitaj.

All of these works combine together to celebrate in symbolic form the nature of a Library as a place of memory and meditation as well as a place of work.

Construction and mechanical engineering

In the ratio of above-ground to below-ground accommodation the building has much in common with an ice-berg: and since the sheer size of the basements required so much excavation special measures had to be taken to minimise disturbance to our major neighbours. In all 250,000 cu.m. of earth was removed. To this end the structural engineers, Ove Arup & Partners, devised the following strategy. First a diaphragm wall of interlocking secant piles alternately reinforced with steel seams was drilled into the ground around the perimeter of the first stage of building. Next, the massive foundations of the original Goods Yard were removed and foundation piles were sunk on a square grid (7.8 m × 7.8 m) to a depth of 35 m. Steel columns were then lowered onto these pile-caps, each column bearing provision for connectors at every basement floor level. Then the topmost (i.e. Piazza) floor slab was cast to form a stiff plate in connection with the columns in such a way that it also acted to prop the top rim of the diaphragm wall. The next move was an operation to dig out the earth beneath the slab like mining sufficiently deep to form shuttering and pour the concrete slab of the first basement. This procedure was repeated progressively for each of the five basement levels building downwards floor by floor. Of course since the

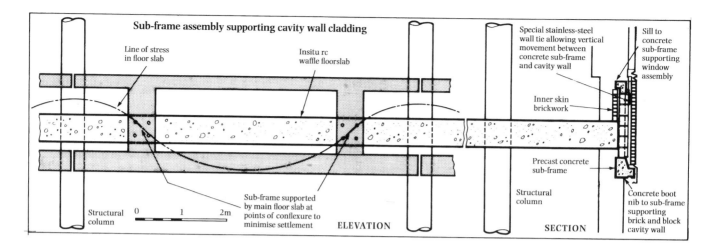

Sub-frame assembly supporting cavity wall cladding

Line of stress in floor slab

Insitu rc waffle floorslab

Special stainless-steel wall tie allowing vertical movement between concrete sub-frame and cavity wall

Sill to concrete sub-frame supporting window assembly

Inner skin brickwork

Structural column

Precast concrete sub-frame

Structural column

Concrete boot nib to sub-frame supporting brick and block cavity wall

Structural column

Sub-frame supported by main floor slab at points of conflexure to minimise settlement

0   1   2m

ELEVATION

SECTION

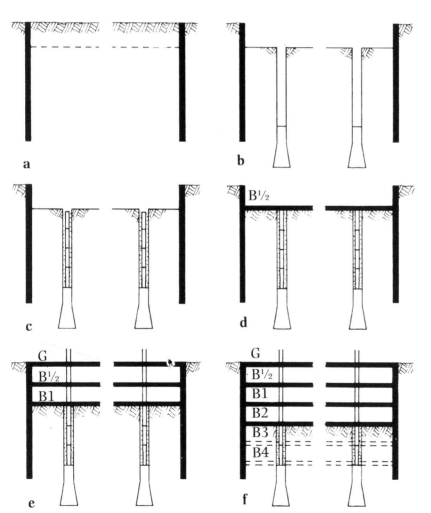

a

b

c

d

B½

G
B½
B1

e

G
B½
B1
B2
B3
B4

f

(*above*) To avoid cracking in the external walls the brickwork is laid in discrete panels on a concrete sub-frame which itself is fixed to the floor slabs at the points of contraflexure. Flexible wall-ties (see right of diagram) allow for differential movement between the sub-frame and the inner cavity wall.

(*left*) Stages in the construction sequence of the basements:

a. The diaphragm wall.

b. Bore-holes for column footings.

c. Steel columns lowered onto the footings.

d. First basement floor is cast.

e. Forecourt and second basement are cast.

f. Process continued to fourth basement while building upwards on the in-place columns proceeds concurrently.

Basement construction. 'Under-reaming' a basement floor-slab and removing the protective corrugated metal lining of the columns to form connections for the next floor-slab. (© Borders/Arup)

columns were all firmly in place it was possible to build the superstructure upwards from them at the same time: we were therefore building upwards and downwards simultaneously.

It was not possible to build deep basements over the central portion of the site because of the traverse of Northern and Central Line tube tunnels. Only one basement could be constructed over this area. Interestingly the concern here was not that the tunnels would be crushed by the weight of the building over but rather that the removal of the weight of excavated earth would result in the tunnels tending to rise! To counteract this tendency a deep concrete slab was laid over the excavation whose boundary wall was retained by ground anchors. (In the event, across the whole width of the site, the tunnels rose by a maximum of 25 mm only.)

Action had also to be taken to mitigate noise and vibration from the Metropolitan and Circle Line tube tunnels being transmitted to the rooms in the Conference Centre. The whole of this portion of the superstructure was therefore mounted on resilient bearings separating it from the substructure.

Typical area of the basement plant room (© Donat)

For the most part the construction of the superstructure was in conventional reinforced concrete frame. However to isolate the brick façade from cracking due to any movement to the floors of the rigid frame the facing bricks were laid on concrete panels which were attached to the frame at two points only of contraflexure and separated by vertical expansion joints with specially moulded bricks to define the expansion joints.

Finally special precautions were taken against rise of ground water by sinking a number of wells and providing an installation for pumping water from the void under the lowest basement.

A building of this size and complexity requires a wide range of mechanical engineering services of all kinds. The design of these was carried out by the firm of Steensen Varming & Mulcahy. These embrace temperature and humidity conditions; circulation installations for both personnel and objects; security control; lighting; sprinkler and other fire fighting systems; plumbing and drainage; alarm and address systems and all other communication systems in addition to the computerized catalogue, request and delivery systems; and mobile stack installations. Half the cost of the building lay in the provision of these services and the 'engine room' is a world of its own covering the greater part of the first basement.

Among all the services perhaps the most important is the control of environmental conditions since the major responsibility of the building is to house and as far as possible extend the life of the nation's heritage of books and manuscripts. Consequently the most valuable items are stored in conditions which minimize the risk of deterioration.

The maintenance of a suitable environment to meet both conservation and occupancy requirements necessitates the use of carefully controlled air-conditioning and lighting throughout the building. The areas of closed-access bookstacks, readers' spaces, offices and public areas each require different environmental control solutions.

I have already described the location of closed-access book storage in three and a half levels below ground. This underground location is in itself conducive to stable and secure storage conditions since the effect of seasonal and diurnal variations in the external temperature and humidity conditions are virtually eliminated. This simplifies the maintenance of a stable internal environment which is vital to the conservation of the material.

There is a maximum temperature variation between the reading and book storage areas of $\pm 3°C$. The design allows for a book storage condition of $17°C$ and 50% RH compared to an above-ground reader area condition of $20°C$ and 60% RH.

The reinforced concrete secant pile wall that surrounds the basements provides considerable mass. When this is taken in conjunction with that of the internal floors, walls and columns and the several thousand tonnes of books and their associated shelving, the enormous thermal storage capacity produced creates an inertia against change in the environmental condition. The air-conditioning system for the basement storage areas is therefore not required to effect any major changes to the total environment but simply to maintain a stable condition.

Methods of fire-fighting were the subject of much research and debate. Hitherto the use of water to put out fire has been a particular anathema to librarians: but ever since it has been found to be practical to freeze damaged material until conservation work can be carried out the use of water has been accepted. The installation of a double action system (in which the overhead dry pipes filled with water when activated by initial alarm sensors and then only discharged when activated by confirmed emergency) was subsequently modified to single action system with pipes constantly filled.

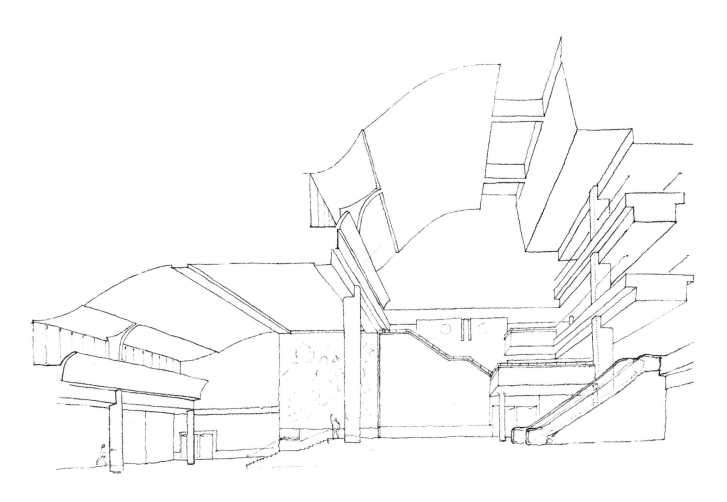

Main Entrance Hall. Drawing ('the big wave') by Wilson.

Postscript

'Those who would carry on great public schemes must be proof against the most fatiguing delays, the most mortifying disappointments, the most shocking insults and worst of all the presumptuous judgement of the ignorant upon their designs.'

(Edmund Burke)

Burke's aphorism was addressed to a community that Napoleon called 'a nation of shopkeepers': and it is by no means irrelevant to our present concern to recall that Napoleon was a bibliophile and avid collector of books who did much to ensure that in French politics culture is a matter of consequence and not, as in England, of condescension. The architectural historian John Summerson once identified as characteristic of British politics 'a national philosophy which expressed itself from time to time in a horrified contempt for architects and architecture'.

In the name of what Kierkegaard so aptly called 'the conceited shrewdness' of 'the practical man' the project has been pulled up by the roots every so often to see if it was still alive, topped and tailed and then shoved back into the ground to test its fitness for survival. Furthermore the rational concept of 'ring-fencing' the finances of a special project – particularly when it is a once-in-a-century undertaking – was never acceptable to the Treasury mentality. As a result all allocation of money whatsoever became the source of bitter resentment from the other national galleries and museums who believed that the money had been appropriated from their budget – certainly a masterly case of divide-and-rule.

The way the British go about making a monument is indeed a sad familiar tale. Wren, on half pay for ten years and sacked before the completion of St Paul's; Disraeli, when Prime Minister, pronouncing that the architect of the Houses of Parliament, Barry, should be hanged in public as an example to the profession: and Street, architect of the Law Courts, hounded to death by constant changes of instruction, overwork and abuse from an odious task master of the Treasury ... And the quality of public 'debate' that is well exemplified by the 'critic' who warned against construction of the Crystal Palace on the grounds that its visitors would go bright red like tomatoes has always favoured the amateur rather than the dreaded expert. In the light of such precedents as these the treatment meted out, over the last thirty-six years, to the building of the British Library, has been, you might say, 'par for the course': but for those who believe that the Library is the one last possession of Great Britain that can justly claim to be 'great' it has been no joke and the outcome, in the terse phrase of Wellington at Waterloo, was 'a damned close-run thing'.

From the time when the first project for this building was launched in 1962 to the time when the last of the reading rooms will be opened in 1999, thirty-seven years will have elapsed. There is no precedent for such a timescale in the genesis of a building until we reach back to the building of St Paul's Cathedral: and even then the longevity of the realization was due more to the nature of traditional building methods than to the irresolution of authority that has dogged the course of our project. Slow progress towards an agreed end is one thing; it is quite another to experience constant change (of site, of funding, of supervising authority, of scale of operation) without any assurance of continuity. For that, I believe, there is no precedent.

However this inordinate prolongation of the process has not been without its advantages. A well-rehearsed brief and two 'dummy runs' at its realization afforded priceless opportunity to ponder the primary themes and to perfect the working details for what in reality had to be a process much like the unfolding of a huge novel, a process that exacted a 'modus operandi' uniquely adapted to shifts in tactic, revision of priorities, assimilation of new evidence, new regulations, new technical processes, a need above all to keep open to change without losing grip on the underlying concept.

It is the peculiar nature of this building that it has already had to assimilate factors of change and growth and, since its life expectancy is of the order of two hundred years, will need to continue doing so over a very long period of time. It is therefore quite natural that this fact should be reflected in both its genesis and its form, but it is also crucial that this process should be able to continue – at least within the scope of those particular requirements identified in the original Brief which are still seen to be essential to the 'critical mass' of the Library. This can only be done on condition that the vacant land which lies to the north of the first phase of the building should be retained. It was expressly acquired for this purpose in the first place since the whole move to St Pancras was determined by the fact that the Bloomsbury site was not big enough. The suggestion that this land should simply be sold off is no less than, in the biblical phrase, 'to sell ones birthright for a mess of pottage' – an example of the 'unthinkable' that is unspeakable.

Among the many advantages accruing from the computerization of the catalogue and request system is the ease with which the demand for every single item can be rationally monitored. This means that material that has the lowest level of demand could be outhoused at Boston Spa (for recall within twenty-four hours). However the Collections will continue to grow apace and the facilities for readership, public access and care of the Collections will also need to evolve and where necessary grow. A great library is like a coral reef whose exquisite structure as it grows proliferates a living network of connections; and its ramification is all of a piece like knowledge itself that bridges the endless curiosity of the human mind, from the first pictogram to the latest microchip. It is of its essence that it grows.

Acknowledgements

Although I am the only actor in this saga who can claim involvement right from the beginning in 1962 it is obvious that such a project could only succeed through the commitment of a large design team drawing upon a range of related disciplines. While the three other Partners in my Firm who saw the St Pancras project through to the finish were all party to every major decision in the politics and management of the project each of us had a particular area of specialization relating to the task as a whole. (At times of black humour we likened ourselves to four paratroopers, back to back, easing our way forward over a minefield!…) The more individual sectors of responsibility fell out as follows: for client liaison and overall design work with me, M. J. Long: for production drawings, programming and co-ordination of consultants, John Collier: for superintendence of all work carried out on site, John Honer. Two other Partners made a considerable contribution in earlier days – Douglas Lanham above all to the building construction at St Pancras up to 1991 and Peter Carolin to the Bloomsbury project for the British Library. A number of Associates made a great personal commitment to the St Pancras building: John Barrow, Alison Bell, Peter Brough, Peter Denney, Dennis Dornan, Brian Frost, Clive Hogben, Rolfe Kentish, Linda Suggate, Fritz Stoll, David Wares. Over fifty assistant architects worked on the project and of these the following made an extended contribution; John Bushell, Hilsie Clelford, Mark Davies, Camillo Gonzalez-Ordonaz, Helen Grassly, Simon Horner, Krzysztof Jaraczewski, Dennis Jordaan, Tony Pryor, Phil Russen, Catherine Stewart, Peter Wong. Project Secretary: Jean Ward with the assistance of Marian Harris, Anne Browning and Jane Powell.

The Structural Engineers were Ove Arup & Partners in whose organization major responsibility fell to: Duncan Michael, John Borders, David Croft, Peter Evans, Stan Januszewski, Ian McVitty, Peter Ryalls, Tony Stevens.

Mechanical engineering services were supplied by Steensen Varming & Mulcahy with major contributions from: Michael Carver, Poul Hansen, Dusan Markovic, David Sworder, David Liptrot, Steve Taylor, who were supported by many engineers of all disciplines.

The firm of Davis Langdon & Everest provided the services of Quantity Surveyor and the particular members of their team were: Nick Davis, Tony Kemp, Sam Mackenzie, Doug Pearce, Roger Roodhouse.

Project management consultants. Schal Project Management, Tim Hare.

Artists and craftsmen. Tapestries, R. B. Kitaj and The Edinburgh Tapestry Company Ltd. Portico Gate, David Kindersley, Lida Cardozo. The readers chair and Boardroom furniture, Ron Carter. Piazza sculpture, Sir Eduardo Paolozzi and Morris Singer Foundry. Signage, Pentagram Design Ltd, Richard Conn, Elizabeth Burney-Jones, Bruce Nivison, Rivermeade Signs Ltd. Exhibition display, Ivor Heal Design, Ronayne Design.

Contractors for the building. Phase 1A, Laing Management Contracting Ltd. Completion phase, McAlpine/Haden Joint Venture.

Appendix: some facts and figures

Key dates

1972	The British Library created by Act of Parliament
1976	St Pancras site bought, and design for the new building initiated
1978	Detailed planning consent and Royal Fine Art Commission approval
1980	First stage of construction approved by Government
1984	Excavation of the basements and work on the superstructure started
1997	First reading room opened
1998	Public opening

Reading rooms

Rare Books & Music	Humanities 2	Science 1 Patents
Manuscripts	Maps	Science 2 Science & Technology
Humanities 1	Oriental & India Office Collections	Science 3 Business

Features

- Desk sizes:

Standard $0.76 \times 1.14\,m$ Manuscripts $0.90 \times 1.14\,m$ Maps $1.11 \times 2.00\,m$

- Each desk is provided with sockets for power supply and other services, and connections to the Online Catalogue (OPAC). Readers are notified that material is awaiting collection by means of a sign lit at the desk.
- Chairs, made from oak and leather to a special design, are interchangeable between reading rooms.
- Carrels in all reading rooms with facilities for word-processors and other equipment.
- Facilities for listening points and other access to National Sound Archive collections.

Storage

- 340 km of shelving, of which more than 240 km is mobile, and the bulk of which is situated in the four storage basements.
- The King's Library occupies 2,438 linear metres of shelving.
- As well as shelving for books, special storage provision is made for microforms, sound recordings, maps, philatelic items, document seals, scrolls, works of art, photographs and other categories of material.

Automated systems

- The Online Catalogue (OPAC) provides access to machine-readable versions of the major British Library catalogues. At least 6.25 million records are searchable in total, the number always increasing. At least 400 reader terminals are placed in the reading rooms.
- The Automated Book Request System (ABRS), accessible through the OPAC terminals, enables requesters to place orders for delivery of material held in closed-access storage areas.
- The Mechanical Book Handling System (MBHS) transports collection items between lower-level bookstores and reading rooms/offices. Target delivery time is within 30 minutes of the order being placed. Actual travel time for an item is between 6 and 15 minutes under normal conditions.

Building Services

- The Building Energy Management System (BEMS) provides some 5,700 monitoring points, and is used to control energy in the building. This is believed to be the largest single-site system in the UK.
- The building is air-conditioned to control temperature, humidity and atmospheric pollutants. The system is designed to meet the following conditions:

	Summer temp (°C)	Winter temp (°C)	Rel.humidity (%)
Reading rooms	21 ±1	21 ±1	50 ± 5
Offices	22 ± 1	20 ± 1	55 ± 5
Entrance Hall	25 max	18 min	Variable
Bookstores	17 ± 1	17 ± 1	50 ± 5
Conference Centre	22 ± 1	20 ± 1	50 ± 5
Exhibition cases	Adjusted locally		

- A computer controlled system maintains different lighting regimes within the building. Artificial light is augmented by natural light in above-ground office areas and reading rooms. Ultra-violet light is excluded wherever possible. Lighting levels range from 45–60 lux in closed-access bookstores to 350 lux in staff areas and reading rooms. Exhibition cases are illuminated at optimum levels by means of a fibre-optic installation.
- Fire protection in every room in the building is provided by a Fire Alarm and Detection System (FADS), which includes nearly 4,000 smoke detectors. The sprinkler system is a 'wet' pipe system.
- 'Floor boxes' are provided at frequent intervals in the platform flooring to allow easy connection to power supply, telephones and ADP systems.
- Public and staff restaurants have seating for c.290 people. The public coffee bar has c.40 seats.
- The building complies with BS5810: Access for the Disabled.

Statistical information

Reader and catalogue desks	Total for all reading rooms	1,277
Number of items held in building	Books and serial volumes	c.12 million
	Patents	c.33 million
	Map items	c.2 million
	Manuscripts	c.0.3 million
	Music scores	c.1.5 million
	Other collections	many millions
British Library staff	(in the building)	c.1,200
Shelving	Total	340 km
Site area:	Building	c.3.1 hectares
	Remaining land	c.2.0 hectares
Gross floor area	Total	112,643 sq m
Floor area, specific functions	Entrance Hall	c.2,650 sq m
	Exhibitions	c.1,350 sq m
	All reading rooms	c.13,000 sq m
	All offices	c.12,000 sq m
Building height above ground	Central flue (=highest point)	47.07 m
	East side superstructure	41.38 m
	West side superstructure	32.35 m
Depth below ground	At lowest point	24.53 m
Site dimesions	Euston Road frontage	84 m
	Ossulston Street frontage	182 m
	Midland Road frontage	172 m
Number of floors	Above ground	9
	Below ground	5½
Internal column grid	Column to column distance	7.8 m
	Area within 4 adjacent columns	60.8 sq m
Floor to ceiling height	Above ground	2.61 m
	In basements	3.35 m
Platform floor	Depth	100–125 mm
Suspended ceiling	Depth	805 mm
Floor loadings	Below ground	14 kN/sq m
	Superstructure	7 kN/sq m
Number of lifts	Total (arranged in 29 sets)	38
Number of toilet areas	Total	71
Building materials	Welsh slates	c.50,000
	Bricks	c.10 million
	Steel reinforcement	c.150,000 tonnes
	Concrete	c.180,000 tonnes

Photographic credits

The author and publishers are very grateful to the following for giving permission to reproduce photographs in this book:

John Borders / Ove Arup, London

Martin Charles, London

John Donat, London

Peter Durant, London

Sir Norman Foster OM, London

Michael Freeman, London

Chris Gascoigne, London

M. J. Long, London

Mainstream, London

Nick Meers, London

Irene Rhoden, London

Steinkamp / Ballog, Chicago

Union Railways, London

Professor Colin St John Wilson RA, London

First published 1998
by The British Library
96 Euston Road, St Pancras,
London NW1 2DB

© 1998 in text Colin St John Wilson

Reprinted, with corrections, 1999

British Library Cataloguing in Publication Data is available from The British Library

ISBN 0 7123 0658 7

Designed and typeset by James Shurmer

Printed and bound in Great Britain at the University Press, Cambridge